THE SOUTHWEST CENTER SERIES

Bernard L. Fontana

EDITOR

Ignaz Pfefferkorn, *Sonora: A Description of the Province*

Carl Lumholtz, *New Trails in Mexico*

Buford Pickens, *The Missions of Northern Sonora: A 1935 Field Documentation*

San José de Tumacácori (Arizona), in 1929. Mission church from the southeast.

The Missions of Northern Sonora

A 1935 Field Documentation

HISTORICAL AND
ARCHAEOLOGICAL ASPECTS

Arthur Woodward

Integrated with
THE ARCHITECTURE

Text and Measured Drawings by
Scofield DeLong and Leffler B. Miller

PHOTOGRAPHS

George Alexander Grant

Edited with preface, notes,
appendices, and references

Buford Pickens, FAIA

THE UNIVERSITY OF ARIZONA PRESS

Tucson & London

Partial funding for this book was provided by the Program for Cultural Cooperation Between Spain's Ministry of Culture and United States' Universities and the Southwest Center of the University of Arizona.

The University of Arizona Press
Copyright © 1993
Arizona Board of Regents
All Rights Reserved

♾ This book is printed on acid-free, archival-quality paper.
Manufactured in the United States of America

98 97 96 95 94 93   6 5 4 3 2 1

Library of Congress Cataloging-in-Publication Data

The Missions of Northern Sonora : a 1935 field documentation / edited with preface, notes, appendices and references by Buford Pickens.
      p.   cm.—(The Southwest Center series)
    Includes bibliographical references and index.
    ISBN 0-8165-1342-2 (cloth : alk. paper).—ISBN 0-8165-1356-2
(pbk. : alk. paper)
    1. Pima Indians—Missions. 2. Spanish mission buildings—Pimería Alta (Mexico and Ariz.) 3. Missions—Pimería Alta (Mexico and Ariz.) 4. Tumacácori National Monument (Ariz.) 5. Kino, Eusebio Francisco, 1644–1711. I. Pickens, Buford. II. Series.
E99.P6M57   1993   92-30728
979.1′79—dc20   CIP

British Library Cataloguing-in-Publication Data
A catalogue record for this book is available from the British Library.

To Jenny, Lindsay, and Grigson

Here we have segregated a nicely defined chapter in
American history that is not duplicated elsewhere
in our National Parks System.
(From "The Tumacacori Story," Dr. Carl Russell, 1935)

Contents

List of Illustrations

All photographs are by George Grant unless otherwise noted.
Abbreviations: WACC, Western Archeological and Conservation Center,
National Park Service, Tucson; AHS, Arizona Historical Society, Tucson.

Chapter 4. Nuestra Señora del Pilar y Santiago de Cocóspera

Foreword

*Where is there a book from which
I can learn about the architecture
of these incredible missions?
There is none.*

Only now, there is.

The Sonoran Desert, which is divided by the United States and Mexican boundary, plays host to some of the most beautiful and otherwise intriguing Spanish-period missions in these two countries. On the Arizona side they are missions San Xavier del Bac, San José de Tumacácori, Los Santos Angeles de Guevavi, and the mission visiting station, or *visita,* of Calabazas. There are other Spanish mission sites in southern Arizona, but these are the only places where structures can now be seen that remain above ground.

San Xavier del Bac continues as an active Indian parish, still serving descendants of the Piman Indians (O'odham) for whom it was founded in the late seventeenth century. Tumacacori is a National Historical Park whose ruins are administered by the National Park Service; Calabazas is the property of the Arizona Historical Society; and Guevavi presently belongs to the Archaeological Conservancy. Federal legislation has mandated that both Guevavi and Calabazas, like Tumacacori, are to come under the care of the National Park Service.

These missions, like their contemporary relatives in neighboring Sonora, were founded in the late seventeenth century by the pioneer missionary in the region, Father Eusebio Francisco Kino, sj. Kino died in 1711, and in 1767 his Jesuit successors were expelled from all of New Spain by edict of King Charles III. The Jesuits were replaced by Franciscan missionaries who arrived on the northern Sonoran scene in 1768. Within a short time, the Franciscans set about to repair Jesuit churches or, in most cases, construct new ones on or near sites where Jesuits had previously built. Before the mid-nineteenth century, the Franciscans were themselves banished from the northern missions—this time by the Republic of Mexico—and both Indian neophytes and buildings were left to fend for themselves as best they could.

The end result of the process begun by Father Kino is seen today in four surviving structures—three as ruins and one intact—in Arizona, and nine in Sonora, three of which are ruins (Cocóspera, Atil, and San Valentín). One of the Sonoran missions, Caborca, is a museum. The others, however, including San Ignacio, Magdalena, Tubutama, Oquitoa, and Pitiquito, remain in use as churches, although their parishioners are now Mexicans rather than Indians. And just as in Arizona, there were other missions which today are no longer visible above ground. These include Mission Dolores, the "Mother Mission" which was begun by Father Kino in 1687 as the first in his circuit and which remained his headquarters throughout the remainder of his life.

Editor Buford Pickens points out that the missions of this so-called "Kino circuit" have received periodic published attention from travelers and from historians, while their archaeological potential and architectural magnificence, especially of those in Sonora, have been largely overlooked. Indeed, their neglect by scholars of art and architectural history is a reflection of a much broader problem, that of the neglect by scholars—with notable rare exceptions—of the art and architecture of the colonial periods for all of Latin America.

The great pioneer of such studies presented in English, Pál Kelemen, has referred to this field as the *Stepchild of the Humanities* (1979). "We are coming slowly to the realization," he writes, "that the Eastern Seaboard, from Massachusetts to Maryland, will never become an advocate for the art of Hispanic America. It is up to those states where young enthusiasts are working, inside or outside the campus, to call attention to the fact that this continent has echoes of the great Spanish past that must be listened to—not with an instrument which has a cracked tuning fork, but with one that can reverberate when it is touched by beauty" (Kelemen 1979, 33).

Much of Kelemen's own scholarly life, spanning more than half a century, has been devoted to an effort to bring light where there has only been darkness, even doing what he can to bring to the attention of a wider public audience some of the mission architectural gems of Sonora, Oquitoa among them (Kelemen 1977, 107–12, Plates 5.24–5.32).

For the early twentieth century, it was the late Herbert E. Bolton who first called the English-speaking public's attention to these remarkable sites. His translation and publication of Kino's *Historical Memoirs of the Pimería Alta* (1919) and his later publication of Kino's biography, *Rim of*

Christendom (1936), reached a wide reading audience and sparked considerable fascination in mission outposts in the northern Sonoran Desert. Bolton, moreover, was never content merely to base his books on research in libraries and archives. He had to see the country for himself. "Retracing the trail" was one of his passions, and beginning in 1909 and continuing sporadically until 1930, he paid several visits to the locales mentioned in the historic documents he was translating. On one of these trips into Kino country, in 1928, he was accompanied by Dean Frank C. Lockwood of the University of Arizona (Bolton 1930, 3: x–xv; Lockwood 1934b, 9–11). Lockwood's enthusiasm led him to mount a second trip to visit the Kino-founded churches, and in the spring of 1928 he led the governors of both Arizona and Sonora on a three-day circuit of the missions. The published result was his book, *With Padre Kino on the Trail* (1934). A second trip, made by him in June, 1932, resulted in another volume, *Story of the Spanish Missions of the Middle Southwest* (1934).

Bolton and Lockwood were not the only persons to visit these places early in the century and to write about them. Theirs, however, are the only early book-length treatments of the subject.

Sometime soon after 1919, Prentice Duell, who had published a book on mission architecture as exemplified by Mission San Xavier del Bac (Duell 1919), visited Sonoran missions. In 1921 he published three articles about them and their Arizona siblings (Duell, "The Arizona-Sonora Chain of Missions"). And at least as early as 1920 the Sonoran missions were visited by Frank Pinkley, Superintendent of Southwestern Monuments of the National Park Service, who was comparing them with Arizona's Mission San José de Tumacácori, which became a National Monument in 1908. Pinkley took photographs of the churches and drew floor plans, both of which are now cared for in the library of the Park Service's Western Archeological and Conservation Center in Tucson, Arizona.

Someone named "A. Trailer," perhaps a nom de plume, took photographs of the church at Altar and the missions at San Ignacio, Magdalena, Caborca, Atil, and Pitiquito and published them along with a brief text in 1921 in a church journal, the *Franciscan Herald* (Trailer 1921). Seven years later, in 1928, Billy Delbridge wrote about his visit to the missions with Dean Lockwood and Arizona Governor G. P. Hunt, publishing it in the *Arizona Historical Review* (Delbridge 1928).

All of these works, like most that have followed, are concerned primarily with the history of the missions rather than with their physical configuration. It was only in 1935 when the National Park Service sponsored an expedition of six professionals to visit the northern Sonoran churches that the first carefully measured plans, preliminary archaeological site surveys, and systematic photographic coverage emerged. They emerged, moreover, in separate reports that were mimeographed or otherwise reproduced in very few numbers for in-house use by the National Park Service. What is ironic is that in spite of the increasing public interest in these now easily accessible missions, no comprehensive study has since been done of the architecture and archaeology of the Sonoran sites. It is only in Magdalena, where the remains of Father Kino were archaeologically uncovered in 1966, that there has been any archaeology at all—and the report of those excavations has yet to see the light of print.

What this means is that the 1935 reports, published together here for the first time, are as timely today as they were when they were written. Moreover, the information they contain, as well as the photographs, provide an excellent baseline from which modern or future studies might proceed. Although there have been many changes in some of the places described, a great deal remains more-or-less intact. Careful study could determine precisely how much.

The 1935 travelers were faced with hardships of the road—not to mention political uncertainties in Mexico—that are difficult for the modern visitor to comprehend. Other than the sites of Dolores, Cucurpe, and San Valentín visited by the 1935 expedition, all the missions are now connected by paved roads and are within easy one-day driving reach of Tucson. Even Dolores, Cucurpe, and San Valentín are not far from paved roads and are readily accessible. All have become popular tourist destinations, a phenomenon fostered in part by publication of such books as Paul Roca's *Paths of the Padres through Sonora* (1967), George Eckhart and James Griffith's *Temples in the Wilderness* (1975), and Charles Polzer's *Kino Guide* (1968) and *Kino Guide II* (1982).

There has also been a plethora of color-illustrated articles concerning these missions in such popular magazines as *Arizona Highways, National Geographic Traveler, Sunset,* and *Tucson Guide* (see, for example, Anonymous 1987; Cheek 1987; Griffith 1989; McDermott 1961; and Thybony 1989). Too, for more than a decade the Southwestern Mission Research Center (SMRC), headquartered in Tucson, has been taking bus loads of visitors to these missions on three-day weekend trips, introducing hundreds of American citizens to their beauty, their history, and to the cultures which fostered them.

It was during an SMRC-sponsored trip in 1983, one whose lecturers were historian/anthropologists Mardith Schuetz and the late Thomas Naylor, that architect and architectural historian Buford Pickens became acquainted with the missions of northern Sonora and southern Arizona. A former president of the Society of Architectural Historians, Pickens was surprised to discover that the architecture of these buildings had not been reported on in any comprehensive manner that was readily available to the public. He subsequently learned about the 1935 National Park Service expedition and its scattered and hard-to-find reports, including the photographs taken by George Grant, and set himself to the task of pulling these materials together into a form suitable for publication as a book. This volume is the result.

Lovers of the Spanish period of history, both documentary and architectural, of Mexico and the United States can be grateful it was Professor Pickens who undertook the job of bringing these reports and photographs to published light. He is a Fellow of the American Institute of Architects; he has been a practicing architect in private practice; he has been Director of the School of Architecture at Tulane University and Dean of the School of Architecture at Washington University as well as a teacher at Ohio University, Wayne State University, the University of Minnesota, and in Florence, Italy; and he has served on committees concerned with the protection of historic buildings in New Orleans, in the State of Missouri, and in St. Louis County, Missouri. He has also had significant involvement with the Historic American Buildings Survey and with the National Trust for Historic Preservation. And, not least of all, he has contributed to three books and is author of nearly four dozen articles on architecture and architectural history published in professional journals.

Having consulted with Professor Pickens on the present project over a period of many years, I can further attest he is a man of bulldog tenacity and determination. While this book is a tribute to the National Park Service personnel who brought the 1935 field expedition to a happy conclusion, so is it a tribute to their latter-day compiler and editor, a retired architect who, appropriately enough, resides in the "Show Me" state, a place further famed for the stubbornness of its mules. Posterity will forever be indebted to Buford Pickens for this labor of his love.

BERNARD L. FONTANA

Editor's Introduction

Americans, as a "nation of transplants," take pride in their cultural origins. They recognize in architecture the visual symbol of their heritage. When we look for the roots of English colonial buildings that remain in Massachusetts or Virginia, we need to visit certain rural counties in England. And for the prototypes of French colonial architecture extant in Louisiana and the Mississippi Valley, we can find many examples along the St. Lawrence River. Still others exist in specific regions of France.

However, in order to study antecedents to the singular blend of Spanish colonial architecture in Arizona, we have only to cross the 1854 Mexican border and travel along the small streams in northern Sonora. Miraculously, many of these part-Spanish, part-Indian, brick and adobe structures from the eighteenth and early nineteenth centuries survive as reminders of a once-thriving "mission community" of Piman Indians (except in Cucurpe, whose natives were Opata-speaking Eudeve Indians).

Additionally, the circuit of missions founded by Father Kino in the late seventeenth century included a few located in what today is southern Arizona. The earliest is Los Santos Angeles de Guevavi, now an adobe ruin. The most famous, and the only one still functioning as a church and which continues to serve Piman Indians, is San Xavier del Bac. The other, made a National Monument in 1908 and now a National Historical Park, is San José de Tumacácori. All were part of the same Piman mission field and all were Jesuit-founded but taken over by the Franciscans after the expulsion of the Jesuits from New Spain in 1767.

Most of the Sonoran historical buildings retain some original architectural elements which, along with a vernacular quality, express the character of their builders. When this evidence of integrity is better known, archaeologists and architectural historians may be motivated to study it "patiently" in the light of closely related, prodigious research.

Since the days of Spanish Borderlands scholar Herbert E. Bolton, two generations of general and religious historians have contributed an outpouring of publications. For architecture, however, there are only a few excellent historical guidebooks, such as Paul Roca's *Paths* (1967), which aid, but do not advance, research on the rich architectural heritage of Sonora.

One notable historian of architecture has called Sonora, which is Mexico's second largest state, "one of the no man's lands of architectural history."[1]

For New Mexico, the seminal works by George Kubler, *Religious Architecture* (1940) and *Mexican Architecture* (1948), provide researchers with an ongoing source of inspiration and a paradigm of method. But, as Kubler admitted, they still leave the architectural study of Sonoran missions for others to pursue "the half-century old, [pioneering] work of our colleagues in 1935."[2]

Many questions remain unanswered about physical aspects of the Sonoran mission complex: its site, extent, design, and construction. Also, a reevaluation of mission architecture in this area is now possible. Today, the design no longer needs to be seen as the provincial attempt at European art historical high style, but rather as "folk culture" (Kelemen 1951, 1: vii, 23; Weismann 1985, 195). And when the field data are available, the missions of Sonora can be appraised with their components, possibly as the communal art of a special people conditioned by their native land, social cohesiveness, and the motivation to build and decorate, taught by a very few inspired padres. Is this a myth, as some insist? Just how did they do it?[3]

The National Park Service Expedition of 1935

Fortunately, more than fifty years ago, the National Park Service (NPS) of the U.S. Department of the Interior, having urgent need for firsthand architectural data in planning the new buildings for Tumacacori National Monument in Arizona, arranged to send an expedition of professional experts to record the remains of twelve missions from the "Kino circuit" missions in northern Sonora.[4] These are the missions established by Jesuit missionary Eusebio Kino in the late seventeenth and early eighteenth centuries in northwestern Nueva Vizcaya, today's northern Sonora and southern Arizona.

Cultural research expeditions that cross international boundaries can be risky ventures, even when government agencies sponsor them. The early 1930s were not the best of times. In Mexico, "Agrarian Reform" under the Revolutionary party had sponsored open anticlerical sentiment. Political and social unrest prevailed in Sonora. Armed conflict was common, street shootings occurred, and churches were being closed under official seals (see notes to chapter 5, n. 4).

In the United States, the Great Depression was giving us the first experiments under the "New Deal" of President Franklin D. Roosevelt. Approval and funding for an expedition to survey missions across the border required a combination of conviction, authority, and luck. Sponsors described it as the "Tumacacori Mission Research Project" and requested seven thousand dollars for funding. It was only at the level of Secretary of the Interior that funding approval could be given, and permission for a party of six professionals to make field studies at isolated mission sites in northern Sonora required permission of the Secretary of State.

In 1935 Professor Bolton was serving on the congressionally mandated Advisory Board of the Secretary of the Interior, a group which advises the Secretary in matters related to the National Parks. His teaching and writing were what inspired members of the expedition to document the physical remains of missions established by Father Kino. Also, it was Bolton who found space for the NPS Field Division of Education to work in Hilgard Hall on the Berkeley Campus of the University of California.

In addition to the men who undertook the 1935 expedition, the names of two individuals within the NPS emerge from the records; their roles were crucial to the project. They had personally previewed the sites in Sonora and provided both paperwork and enthusiastic support for the expedition.

The first of these, Frank Pinkley, was Superintendent of Southwestern Monuments. As early as 1919–20 he realized the vital kinship of the Kino missions in Mexico to those in Arizona. What was then Tumacacori National Monument was one of his responsibilities. In 1920 he made his own exploratory field trip to Sonora, returning with measurements for floor plans and photographs of all the mission churches which he found were related to Arizona examples (Rothman 1989).

Pinkley's 1920 floor plans were recorded on glass negatives and are conserved at the NPS Western Archeological and Conservation Center in Tucson. From 1919 until 1935, Pinkley's annual reports described in graphic detail the repair and stabilization work proceeding at Tumacacori National Monument. He insisted upon planning for a new education and interpretive museum, the design and contents of which would depend upon further field data from Mexico's mission prototypes—to be available "only while they still stand."

The other key role player within the NPS was Carl Parcher Russell, whose official title in 1935 was Chief of the NPS Museum Division within the Branch of Field Research and Education, with an office in Hilgard Hall. Russell, influenced by Bolton and Pinkley, was convinced that even "... leaving out of consideration the international significance of the Tumacacori project, there remains the fact that here we have segregated a nicely defined chapter in American history that is not duplicated elsewhere in our National Parks System" (Russell 1935, 2).

Furthermore, Russell took the preliminary step in planning the 1935 survey by personally making a scouting trip into Sonora during the fall of 1933, along with NPS Park Naturalist Robert Rose, who was assigned the task by Pinkley. During a follow-up visit in the winter of 1934, Russell narrowed the expedition's scope as it was later defined on the application for funds to the National Emergency Council in Washington, D.C. Following his two Mexican trips, Russell wrote "The Tumacacori Story," a report describing the status of Tumacacori in the National Parks System and presenting an outline for further study. Clearly, he was one of the best qualified to cut through bureaucratic red tape. He had expected to go with the 1935 survey team but was transferred to another assignment.[5]

Among non-NPS personnel whose influence was greatest in connection with the project was historian Herbert E. Bolton (1870–1953). The Sonoran survey was planned, researched, and completed on the campus of the University of California at Berkeley where the NPS had found space for its Field Operations Headquarters. Bolton was head of the university's history department. Significantly, in 1919 he had translated Father Eusebio Kino's *Historical Memoir of Pimería Alta* after finding the original 1699–1711 manuscript in Mexican archives and traversing in person the padre's difficult cross-country trails. In 1936, Bolton published his famous biography of Kino, *Rim of Christendom*, a work republished in 1960 and again in 1984. Bolton's involvement with the Secretary of the Interior and his arranging for space in Hilgard Hall have already been mentioned.

In its final form, the expedition consisted of six persons. In addition to Woodward, DeLong, Miller, and Grant, they were Robert Rose, and

J. H. Tovrea, an engineer on Pinkley's staff. Official authorization came from the National Emergency Council via document No. 5546 issued on 15 August 1935. It was described as "The Tumacacori Mission Research Project." In part, the document provided authorization:

> . . . to proceed at once with the important work of collecting architectural data of this [Kino, Pimería Alta] mission group. . . . Preliminary exploration trips have already been made through this territory [field studies in 1933 and 1934 by Carl Russell and Robert Rose] revealing a wealth of architectural detail still preserved on the missions in the same stylistic group as Tumacacori. . . .

Justification:

> This particular project should be viewed in the same light as the measured records of the Historic American Buildings Survey have come to be regarded—invaluable documents preserving for future study and actual restoration data—the exact architectural measured record of the fast disappearing remains of an unique North American architecture.
>
> The value of the records proposed will be enhanced as time goes on and the missions of the Pimería Alta group slowly disappear.[6]

The Reports of the Expedition

The results of the 1935 field documentation were presented to a small NPS audience in three related, but hitherto separate, reports. The first is a sprightly text written with a minimum of NPS federalese by Arthur Woodward (age 37), professional archaeologist and journalist. The second, by two professional architects, Scofield DeLong (age 32) and Leffler B. Miller (age 40), consists primarily of architectural measured drawings (28 sheets of plans and details) together with an outline of descriptive data and field notes made at each mission site. In this book most chapters consist of Woodward's text for a mission site followed by DeLong and Miller's outline description and drawings. Chapters for Altar and Mission Dolores have no outline description; chapters for missions Guevavi and San Xavier del Bac contain outline descriptions but no text by Woodward.

The third report was photographic, one made by a key member of the expedition party, George A. Grant (age 44), then chief NPS photographer who enjoyed a nationwide reputation. Grant took more than 300 photographs. Many of these, most heretofore unpublished, have been selected and keyed here to illustrate the observations of the others. Grant's sharp images supplement both text and drawings, presenting a record of mission buildings as they were in 1935—some now altered and a few in ruins.

All three of these reports contain firsthand, on-site observations, including photographic images and measured data. The two texts add perceptive recommendations, anticipating a systematic follow-up. A few copies of the DeLong/Miller report were mimeographed for in-house use by the NPS, but none of this material has been available to a broader public through responsible publication in English. The DeLong/Miller report, lacking many of the illustrations, was published in Spanish translation in Hermosillo in 1976 by the Centro Regional del Noroeste of the Instituto Nacional de Antropología e Historia as number 21 in its scholarly series, *Cuadernos de los Centros* (DeLong and Miller 1976). And in 1983, recognizing the value of Woodward's report as a primary source, the Governor of Sonora published it in Spanish translation (Woodward 1983). The budget for its publication was limited, however, and it contains only a few poorly reproduced photographs. Additionally, it has had practically no distribution in the United States.

The 1935 mission survey was a coordinated team effort demanding far more time—several months in writing, drafting, and developing—than was taken in the field. This fact, together with the professional quality of the three reports, strongly implied that they should be unified under one title and updated with minimal editorial notes.[7] Later scholarship, as noted, has altered minor details of the original text, but the authors were remarkably on track and, even in their conjectures, going in the right direction.

DeLong and Miller were architects, not historians or archaeologists. They confined their text to a brief, historical handbook summary in order to face their formidable, primary task, which was graphically and accurately to measure and record the plans, sections, and details of as many buildings as possible.

As precedent for their work, the architects cited the publications of another inspired young professional, Prentice Duell (1894–1960). He had published a monograph on *Mission San Xavier del Bac* in 1919 and had followed this book with a series of three articles (Duell 1921). Considering the similarity of subjects and their provenance, Duell's exemplary drawings must have provided an incentive as well as a challenge to DeLong and Miller. They went beyond Duell, however, by including examples that show native influence as well as six plates of ornament in color.

Arthur Woodward had studied under both professors Alfred L. Kroeber, a noted anthropologist, and Bolton. Like Bolton, he also believed that during its heyday the Spanish colonial mission was far more than the church building. His sketches of mission site plans show the archaeologist's curiosity in searching for the foundations of other structures now gone. Did the mission once resemble a *rancho*? Or was it more like a small *pueblo* which housed the Indian neophytes and their daily work places for milling, weaving, baking, blacksmithing, tanning, etc. (Konrad 1980)? Woodward calls attention to the need for research and especially for excavations "properly conducted before we can obtain an adequate picture of the complete mission establishment."

It seems clear from his introduction that Woodward set certain limits for himself in order not to impinge upon the architects' role, with exceptions noted. His primary concern lay beneath the surface. At every site he scouted the terrain looking for clues that might guide later excavations.

The architects, on the other hand, keenly aware of the immediate needs at Tumacacori National Monument, restricted the scope of their recording to specific architectural data. Also, because of the exceptional photographic coverage by George Grant, the architects could omit, as they did except at Caborca, the measurements necessary to draft exterior elevations and, more importantly, longitudinal sections. Mindful of these omissions, Delong and Miller explicitly noted that additional "architectural studies in Sonora would be profitable but are not deemed necessary at this time."

Apparently, both the architects and the archaeologist assumed that early manuscript plans and written records—guidelines pertaining to the first Kino missions, to other pre-1767 Jesuit structures, and to later Franciscan buildings—might someday turn up in Mexican archives, especially after the 1930s era of political unrest. During the intervening half century, however, there still has been no revelation of such records dealing with precepts for mission site selection, design, and construction. Some researchers still look forward to the discovery of such documents; those pertaining to Spanish colonial civil and military establishments seem to be common.

Authors, Photographer, and Other Members of the Expedition Team

Whether by serendipity or design, the selection of the six investigators to conduct the Sonoran mission study for the NPS in 1935 could hardly have been any better. These were people well qualified for the task which lay at hand. Detailed biographical notes for principal members of the team are presented in appendix A.

Results of the 1935 Expedition

The most immediate and tangible result of the 1935 expedition was the construction at Tumacacori of the combination museum-visitor center-office building. Built at a cost of $28,992.91 by M. M. Sundt Construction Company of Tucson, the building was completed in December 1937.

Many authentic architectural quotations came from specific examples that were recorded in Sonora: The shell motif over the main entrance is a copy of that at Mission Cocóspera; the carved wood entrance doors are replicas of those at Mission San Ignacio; the carved corbels and beamed ceiling in the lobby are inspired by those at Oquitoa; the piers and arches in the patio are based on those at Caborca; and the groin-vaulted ceiling in the view room got its inspiration from Tubutama and other Sonoran missions. The wooden grill work on the west office window was copied from the choir loft at Tubutama (Bleser 1989, 41). DeLong's full size details for some of these features are preserved at the NPS Denver Service Center. He served as architect for the building.

Installation of the museum in the new building at Tumacacori began in 1938, the research and assembly having been carried out at the NPS laboratory on the Berkeley campus of the University of California. The museum was finished, including its detailed dioramas, in February 1939 (Bleser 1989, 41).

Throughout the text of their reports the authors, in passing, made frequent references to the remains at Tumacacori which they had studied in preparation for the expedition. Their reports included only a few general photographs. As the research motive, the Arizona mission was uppermost in their minds as they searched for evidence of its architectural relationships in Sonora. Since 1935 much has been written and published about Mission Tumacacori; but also much is out of print. The most recent descriptive monograph is Nicholas J. Bleser's popular historical booklet, *Tumacacori: from Ranchería to National Monument* (1989).

For the benefit of readers who may be unfamiliar with this Kino mission in southern Arizona, or who may need to have some convenient basis at hand for comparison with the Sonoran missions, I append brief descriptive material and related documents on the physical aspects of Tumacacori in appendix B. For further study see Bleser, and other comprehensive works listed in References.

As a result of foresight by the NPS in 1935, the frontier mission complex in Sonora now invites the serious attention, and especially the collaboration, of architectural historians, archaeologists, and others armed with new incentives and evaluation methods from accumulated research in kindred fields, archaeology to folklore.

At the very least, a study of these NPS reports should contribute to a better understanding of the Pimería Alta missions on both sides of the border. We might also hope to learn more about the formative and decorative quality that distinguishes architecture, as material culture, in Piman missions when compared with missions in other regions of the Hispanic Southwest.

BUFORD PICKENS

Acknowledgments

In an era of myriad machine copies often made from carbons, mimeographs, or blueprints, we faced our first problem in editing 1936 manuscripts: to find *original* typescripts, drawings, notes, etc. In this case, where the authors were either deceased or unable to assist in the task, another problem was to identify the genesis and prime movers of the 1935 Mexican expedition. During this search we visited most of the principal NPS archives—regional and national—as well as the National Archives in Washington, D.C., the Bancroft Library at the University of California, and numerous special libraries in Tucson, Arizona.

In January 1985 Lic. Francisco Manzo Taylor of Hermosillo, Sonora, at the request of his friend, Arthur Woodward, sent us a Xerox copy of Woodward's original typescript. Manzo Taylor had used it to translate the text for publication, in Spanish, of Woodward's report as: *Misiones del norte de Sonora: Aspectos históricos y arqueológicos*, Prólogo de Charles W. Polzer (Hermosillo: Gobierno del Estado de Sonora, 1983). Dr. Polzer was helpful in obtaining this authentic Woodward typescript, not available in U.S. archives, for our editing purposes. Also, he kindly provided an English copy of his own *prólogo*.

Dr. Polzer was one of the founders in 1965 of the Southwestern Mission Research Center (SMRC) which has stimulated public interest and carried forward educational and research projects, functioning first at the Arizona Historical Society, subsequently at the Arizona State Museum, and now at the University of Arizona Library. Through its publications, the SMRC provides "a clearinghouse of information for those engaged in, or contemplating research in northern New Spain."

Another most important educational function of SMRC is the spring and fall guided bus tour of the "Kino missions" in Sonora. This three-day "field seminar," in situ, has enabled an interested public to see firsthand the mission churches functioning in their natural setting—"architectural diamonds in the rough." After this experience, participants begin to understand the significance of a long-overlooked chapter in American history. With several other architectural historians, we were privileged to take this tour in spring of 1983 under the well-informed guidance of Dr. Mardith Schuetz-Miller, and the late Thomas H. Naylor, and like many others, we have been inspired to return many times since.

Dr. Bernard L. Fontana, Field Historian at The University of Arizona Library, and Dr. Polzer, sj, Ethnohistorian at the Arizona State Museum at the University, served as dynamos for smrc. Both have taken the time from a myriad of more immediate tasks to encourage the editing of the 1935 field documentation of the Sonoran missions. Dr. Schuetz-Miller and the late Thomas H. Naylor, also affiliated with smrc, aided materially in the editing process.

Over a period of three years, through correspondence, and in person, I tested the patience of countless library staff members in the National Park Service across the country. To them are owed my thanks for their indulgence and help. Especially cited for their individual aid are Edwin C. Bearss, Chief Historian, nps, Washington, D.C.; John B. Clonts, Chief, Division of Anthropological and Library Collections, Lynn M. Mitchell, Photo-Archivist, and Mark Sawyer, photographer, all presently or formerly at the nps Western Archeological and Conservation Center, Tucson, Arizona; David Nathanson, Chief Librarian, and Ruthanne Heriot, Special Collections Librarian, nps Harpers Ferry Center, West Virginia; Hal Rothman, historian in Santa Fe, New Mexico; James W. Troutwine, Superintendent, Tumacacori National Historical Park and Nicholas J. Bleser, the dedicated and many-talented Park Ranger at Tumacacori. It was he who first suggested the simple logic, "just to publish the Woodward and DeLong-Miller reports together, as one" historical document.

Throughout the editing, personal correspondence with, and study of publications by John L. Kessell have kept the project on track. Friends of Arthur Woodward, Al Schroeder, J. Bankston, and his former students Drs. Barbara A. Tyler and Sandra L. Myres, gave material aid and encouragement.

Last, but far from least, I am beholden to my son Lindsay, Capt. usaf Ret., computer specialist, who several times aided my visits to the mission sites and later synchronized the software, hardware, and diskettes, sine qua non.

THE MISSIONS OF NORTHERN SONORA

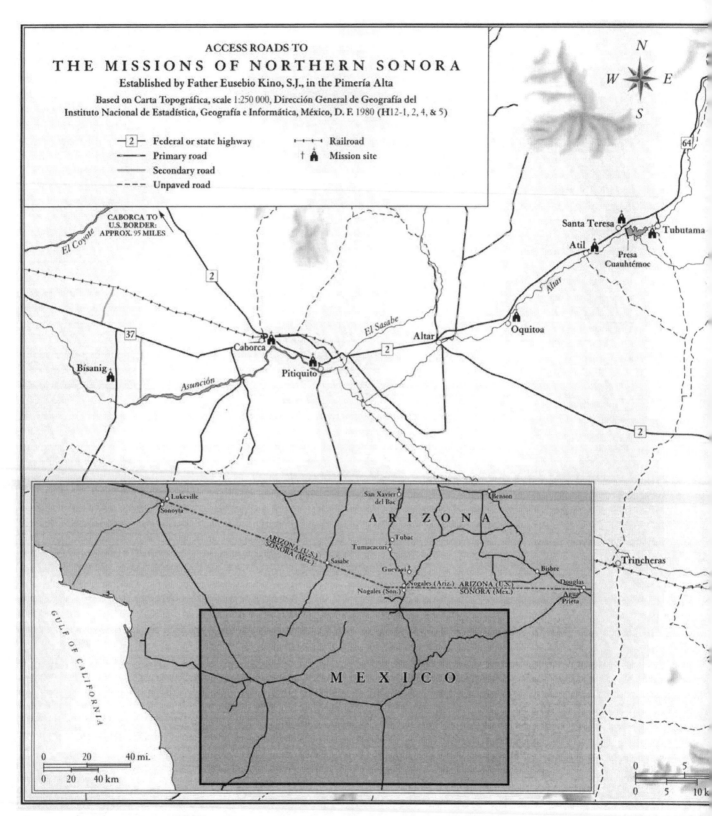

ACCESS ROADS TO

THE MISSIONS OF NORTHERN SONORA

Established by Father Eusebio Kino, S.J., in the Pimería Alta

Based on Carta Topográfica, scale 1:250 000, Dirección General de Geografía del
Instituto Nacional de Estadística, Geografía e Informática, México, D. F. 1980 (H12-1, 2, 4, & 5)

Federal or state highway	Railroad
Primary road	Mission site
Secondary road	
Unpaved road	

CABORCA TO
U.S. BORDER:
APPROX. 95 MILES

El Coyote

Santa Teresa
Atil
Tubutama
Presa
Cuauhtémoc

Altar

37

Caborca
Pitiquito
Altar
Oquitoa

Bísanig

Asunción

ARIZONA

Lukeville
Sonoyta

San Xavier
del Bac
Benson

ARIZONA (U.S.)
SONORA (Mex.)
Sasabe

Tubac
Tumacacori
Guevavi

Bisbee

Trincheras

Nogales (Ariz.)   ARIZONA (U.S.)
Nogales (Son.)   SONORA (Mex.)

Douglas
Agua
Prieta

GULF OF CALIFORNIA

MEXICO

| 0 | 20 | 40 mi. |
| 0 | 20 | 40 km |

| 0 | | 5 |
| 0 | 5 | 10 k |

Access roads to the missions.

15

2

Cocóspera

Cocóspera

Cananea

2

Imuris

2

Remedios

San Ignacio

Magdalena

Magdalena

15   2

Santa Ana

Dolores

15

Cucurpe

mi.

Map produced by Ortelius Design.

CHAPTER ONE

Authors' Introductions

Historical and Archaeological Aspects

The primary object of the Sonora expedition was to obtain architectural and historic data which might furnish studies for the possible restoration[1] of portions of the Tumacacori National Monument, one of the Kino missions chain, and which would enable the architects and museum technicians to make more accurate exhibits for the new museum projected for Tumacacori.

The work of assembling the various data was apportioned among members of the party as follows: Architectural studies by Leffler Miller and Scofield DeLong (elected chief of the party), assisted by Howard Tovrea, engineer attached to the Southwestern Monuments Headquarters, and Robert Rose, Park Naturalist, likewise from Southwestern Monuments Headquarters, George Grant, official photographer for the National Park Service, and Arthur Woodward, archaeologist-historian and interpreter (Fig. 1.1) [cf. Fig. 14.3].

Two cars were used, one belonging to the National Park Service Branch of Plans and Design in San Francisco, and the other operated by George Grant, who carried the luggage.

STARTING OUT UNDER MARTIAL LAW

Owing to rumors of trouble in the region in which we wished to work, it was deemed necessary to proceed to Hermosillo in order to obtain an official permit from the governor of the state. This proved to be a wise move.[2]

There was some unrest in the region of Magdalena, Santa Ana, and Altar (Fig. 1.2). The *presidente* and the chief of police of Santa Ana were

FIGURE I.I. Members of the Sonora Expedition at the start. Left to right: Rose, Woodward, DeLong, Tovrea, Miller, and Grant.

seized and shot early in the morning of 13 October 1935 (the day after we arrived at Hermosillo). Immediately, we heard stories of other atrocities but, aside from the shooting affair in Santa Ana, no other fatalities occurred in the region in which we worked. We traveled all through the disaffected area but were unhindered in our work and received only the most courteous treatment from the officials and townspeople.

Detachments of the Sixteenth Infantry and the Twenty-sixth Cavalry of the Federal Army were on duty in Hermosillo, Nogales, Magdalena, Santa Ana, and later at Altar. Owing to the unrest in those towns, the secretary of the governor (the latter being out of town) suggested that for the peace of all concerned we remain in Hermosillo for a day or so, until the troops could take control of the towns and restore order. Not being cognizant of the true state of affairs, and wishing to abide by the wishes of the government, we concluded to do so. On the morning of the sixteenth the secretary wrote out a *permiso* for us; armed with this we left Hermosillo for Magdalena, which city we planned to use as a base of operations for a survey of missions San Ignacio, Cocóspera, and Magdalena.

SCOPE OF THE SURVEY

In describing our operations at the various missions I shall limit myself to a discussion of the condition of the missions at the present time, giving only a résumé of the historic settings and taking them in the order in which we approached them. I shall not attempt a detailed description of

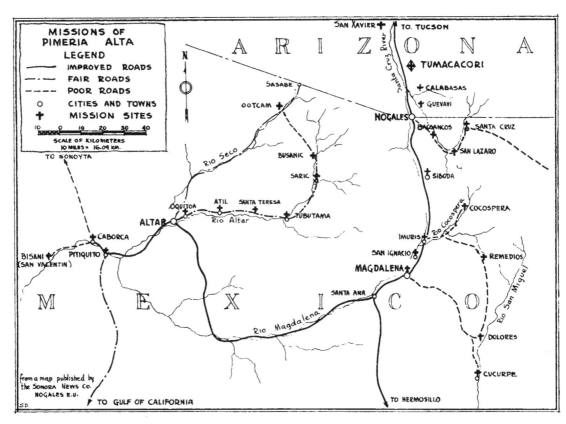

FIGURE I.2. Map (1935). Itinerary of
the Expedition showing missions visited
(DeLong).

the architectural features, leaving that to the members of the party who
were directly concerned with such work. Only in such places where I
deem it necessary to point out possible reconstruction in connection with
historic events and the evidence substantiating such reconstruction shall I
attempt any discussion of such features.[3]

To obtain a proper perspective on the problems of the Sonora missions
and their architecture, it is necessary to call attention to certain fundamen-
tal historical, archaeological, and ethnological facts. It is not my intention
to delve deeply into the various phases of the historical background of
missionary work in Sonora and Arizona. Such a study would demand too
much time, and the result would be a series of volumes rather than a
report. On the other hand, some explanation of certain factors is deemed
necessary. I shall limit myself to a brief exposition of the Indians of the
region involved, with a general review of events which took place in the
founding of the missions under discussion, and also something of the sub-
sequent history of the mission establishments after their cession to the
Franciscans by the Jesuits.

Unfortunately, our knowledge of the Franciscan occupation of Sonora and Arizona is rather meager.[4] No doubt there are reams of original documents touching upon this subject, but we have very little that has been compiled with any degree of authority.

Concerning the actual construction of the missions proper, and the periods in which they were built, our information is practically nil.[5] Only from a few sources do we obtain firsthand glimpses of the structures as they were being made ready for occupancy. Our knowledge must be gleaned from scattered references and from later observations by travelers. It is possible that this combined report will serve as the first technical or semi-technical discussion of the architectural phases of construction of these missions.

A few years ago, in 1921, Prentice Duell, architect, wrote a series of articles, "The Arizona-Sonora Chain of Missions." More recently in 1934, Dr. Frank C. Lockwood published his *Missions of the Middle Southwest*. The latter is somewhat in the nature of a guidebook indicating where these missions are located and how to reach them. Duell's report is more to the point, but he omits many features desirable in such a record.[6]

We realize that in this report, also, much has been left out—many questions remain unanswered—all of which is to be expected when one considers that we remained in Mexico only from 12 October to 29 October. Aside from making the roughest of measurements and sketches, we were unable to excavate or otherwise thoroughly to explore the mounded ruins for the evidence necessary to make qualified statements. No accurate account of this mission chain will ever be written until the trowel and brush of the historical archaeologist lays bare the old floors and walls, and he examines the crumbling debris on the mission sites proper to make a thorough intelligent reconnaissance of the native Indian sites in the region.

THE NATIVE POPULATION

It is not my intention to dwell at length upon the ethnology of the Indians of this region. This has been done by several authors, the last compilation having been made in 1934 by Dr. Ralph Beals under the heading, "Material Culture of the Pima, Papago and Western Apache." However, one or two points should be mentioned in connection with the native inhabitants which have not been previously considered.

Scattered throughout the Altar, Magdalena, and San Miguel river valleys are numerous hills upon which occur small terraced places supported by stone walls. These are known as "*trincheras*." Upon these small platforms which cling to the steep slopes overlooking fertile agricultural flats,

Indians once built their homes. I do not believe these natives have been accurately identified with any one of the present tribes. However, from the types of the pottery which exist on such trincheras and also on the sites of the missions proper, there seems some reason to believe that possibly these places were occupied during mission times. Indeed, they may have supplied neophytes to Oquitoa, Santa Teresa, Imuris, San Ignacio, Tubutama, Dolores, and perhaps others. A small type collection of shards bearing a purplish micaceous paint, identified as "Trincheras ware" and commonly thought of as being associated with the trincheras proper, was brought back from the missions mentioned.

Any future research into the mission problem in Sonora should include a brief survey of certain of the trincheras which are found in closest association with the missions. One such site is on the low hill directly across from Oquitoa.[7]

The reason for stressing the native population of Sonora in connection with the mission chain is obvious. No mission was ever constructed in a land barren of Indians. The missions existed by, and for the Indians. No mission could have been erected without Indian labor, and no fields tilled without neophytes, and the large herds of horses, mules, cattle, and sheep would have gone untended without the aid of native herders. It was the wild enemy tribes of the Apache and rebellious Pima who rose against the missions. For these reasons the Indian should play a major part in the story, and we should have as much information concerning him as it is humanly possible to obtain in order to complete our understanding of the missions and their problems.

As Dr. Beals so aptly states, "Perhaps no region of North America is so little known to the anthropologist as northern Mexico between the American border and a line drawn from the mouth of the Río Pánuco to the southern boundary of Jalisco" (Beals 1932).

However, in considering the native population in this report it will not be necessary to include the territory south of the Altar River, nor east of the Río San Miguel.

In the main, the tribes centering around the missions of the Pimería Alta, or the Upper Pima country, consisted of the Pima, Papago, and the northernmost division of the Opata on the Río San Miguel.

Usually the Pima and the Papago are considered the same stock with but minor variations in material culture and dialectic differences in language. Concerning the latter it may be mentioned that in southern Arizona, south of the present town of Casa Grande—in a rather narrow strip of territory dividing the area, claimed by the present-day Pima and

Papago—lives a small group of people known as the Cojate or *Quahadike*. These people have been noticed from the earliest times as a separate unit, yet when one examines the truth of the matter it becomes only too apparent that the Cojate are composed of the Pima-Papago stock. As a Pima expressed it, "They are half-and-half people. Pima man he marry Papago woman, they live there. Papago man marry Pima girl, they live there. They Cojate."[8]

In other words, the linguistic differences and the feeling between the two tribes have been sufficient to create a separate division. Then, too, there are minor differences in the material culture such as basketry, some pottery, household utensils, and ceremonies. To what extent these differences existed in the early historic or late prehistoric times is difficult to state.

In Sonora proper the Papago now inhabit the territory which was termed the Pimería in mission days. This is particularly true of the district west of the Altar River. The lands surrounding San Xavier del Bac [near Tucson] from which Kino drew his workmen for his missions of Cocóspera and Remedios were then Pima. Today they are Papago territory. Early writers have divided the Pima-Papago on linguistic and material cultural differences, maintaining that the Papago were lower in the cultural scale. Whether this was actually true is difficult to determine. The Pima call themselves *A-a-tam* meaning simply "the people." Papago means "bean-people" and is derived from the words *papah* (beans) and *Ootam* (people). In the latter word is seen the resemblance to A-a-tam, the true name of the Pima (Hodge, 2:200, 251).[9]

ARTHUR WOODWARD

The Architecture

The problems of stabilization, reconstruction, and restoration together with proposals for a museum and exhibits at Tumacacori National Monument have raised numerous questions involving the architecture and history of this famous Arizona mission. The answers to many of the questions are to be found in a study of the missions established in the late seventeenth and early eighteenth centuries by Padre Eusebio Kino, which for the most part lie in Sonora, Mexico. The [primary] purpose of the Sonora expedition was to make a preliminary survey of these missions, securing architectural and historical data which will aid the architects and museum technicians in the solutions of these problems.[10]

Members of the expedition were: Howard Tovrea, Chief Engineering Aide, and Robert Rose, Park Naturalist, both from the Southwestern Monuments Headquarters; George Grant, official photographer of the National Park Service; Arthur Woodward, Associate Laboratory Technician [in history and archaeology]; Leffler Miller, Associate Architect from the Field Division of Education; and Scofield DeLong, Associate Architect representing the Branch of Plans and Design, who was in charge of the party (see Fig. 1.1 above).

Permission to pass into Mexico, with two U.S. government [NPS] cars and the necessary cameras and equipment, was secured from the Chief of Customs at Nogales, Sonora, through the offices of the American consul. We proceeded directly to Hermosillo, the capital of Sonora (see Fig. 1.2 above), where we visited the secretary of the governor, securing there an official permit to carry on our mission studies. This procedure proved to be indispensable for the successful completion of our work. The Mexican officials were most courteous.

Our entrance into Sonora preceded by only a few hours an uprising in this area during which a few well-aimed assassin's shots deprived us of the privilege of meeting several of the town officials and caused us to remain at the Hotel Ramos in Hermosillo longer than we had planned!!! We were, however, well protected since the governor and his bodyguard were stopping here, which allowed us to sleep peacefully behind thick walls while machine gun artists stomped quietly past our doors all night long [cf. Woodward's introduction, pp. 1–2].

The uprising having degenerated into a game of hide and seek between the soldiers and the rebels—with a sideline of "horse borrowing"—we proceeded to carry on our studies of all the important mission sites. These studies were necessarily brief and consisted of taking photographs, making as many architectural drawings and sketches as time would permit, and taking notes on the construction and detail.

These missions were established by Jesuit Padre Kino between 1687 and 1711 and operated by the Jesuits until their expulsion from Mexico in 1767. However, the churches as they stand today are, in general, Franciscan structures or Franciscan reconstruction of Jesuit buildings.

The architectural drawings included in this report are compiled from the notebooks of Leffler Miller and Scofield DeLong. Howard Tovrea's contributions along this same line having been incorporated, for the most part, in his report on Tumacacori, submitted 15 January 1936 [see appendix B, pp. 157–162]. These drawings depict the different types of mission planning, construction detail, ornament, and furnishings, but all are not necessarily accurate, as many sites had to be covered in a comparatively short time, thus precluding the possibilities of checking for accuracy.

The architectural photographs herein were taken by Leffler Miller, the numerous excellent photographs by George Grant being on file in Washington, D.C.[11] Arthur Woodward's ability as an archaeologist and interpreter proved invaluable to the party. Robert Rose, having previewed most of the Sonora mission sites in 1934 with Dr. Carl Russell, contributed much toward the success of the expedition.

MATERIALS AND CONSTRUCTION

The materials used in erecting the missions were those available near the sites. Stones of varying degrees of durability and quality are found throughout Sonora, the stones employed in the buildings being, for the most part, small and easily handled. In the construction of San Xavier del Bac in Arizona, however, stone had to be transported many miles from the nearest mountains, the Indian women carrying these stones on their heads the entire distance, no stone being allowed to touch the ground until the mission site was reached.[12]

Clay used in the making of burned brick is readily obtainable throughout the area. The bricks are soft but durable, and a dull red in color. The sizes and shapes vary, some at Caborca measuring 8″ x 8″ x 1-1/4″ for the vaulted ceiling construction, and 8″ x 10″ x 2-1/2″ for piers and walls, while others at Oquitoa measure 6″ x 12″ x 1-3/4″.

Adobe, a material widely used in the Southwest, played a very important part in mission construction. The idea of using adobe bricks was imported to Mexico from Spain where it had been used as a building material since the advent of the Moors. These sun-dried bricks were made in various sizes, from 2″ to 4″ thick and from 12″ to 18″ long. Straw, twigs, and stone particles were used as a bond and provided a material quite durable when properly protected.

Wood was employed for roof beams, lintels, doors, and furniture. Mesquite and pine were mostly used, mesquite being the most common in Sonora. The *vigas* (beams) found in most of the missions had been adzed square, but in some cases as at Oquitoa, round logs had been used along with the squared beams.

Window and door openings are commonly spanned with wood lintels. These members are plastered over, first being scored to form a better bond enabling the plaster to adhere. In the older structures the window consisted of a wood frame in which vertical wood bars were placed to form a wood grille. Behind the wood grille, solid wood shutters swing on wood

FIGURE 1.3. San José de Tumacácori, looking up into unfinished bell tower.

pins. An excellent example of this type of window was found in the old adobe wall of Cocóspera. Only the frame remained, but the window is easily reconstructed from this as illustrated in the detail drawings of Cocóspera (see below, Fig. 4.III).

Doors were of two types, the simpler type being built of wood planks on wood frame; the more elaborate doors being paneled. The older doors are pivoted, wood pins or pivots at the top and bottom being inserted in round holes provided in the head and sill of the door frame. Doors were also found which hung on iron pins inserted in the side of the opening. More elaborate hardware consisting of iron hinges and locks was provided for some of the later doors.

Wood choir-loft rails, for the most part, had wood balusters turned on a lathe. Probably some of these early types were made on primitive lathes operated by neophytes. At Tubutama we saw the oldest rail, consisting of heavy, hand-carved balusters, undoubtedly the work of the Indian (see Fig. 13.I).

Saguaro cactus ribs, cane, and ocotillo, also had a part to play in the mission construction. Similar to small round poles, they were laid over the vigas and in every case at a right angle to the vigas, to form the finished ceiling.

Structural systems were of two types, the post-and-lintel, and the arch-and-pier. A third system, the truss, does not appear in the Sonora missions. Although we found a pitched roof with wood rafters at Cocóspera, the builders made no attempt to construct a real truss.

Little is known of the construction of the first temporary quarters at the mission sites. They may have been similar to those erected in California which were little better than brush huts, more livable quarters later being constructed of wood posts set closely together and plastered inside and out with clay, and roofed with poles, grass, and mud.

Adobe brick construction was taken up as a more permanent type of construction. The bricks when dried were laid up in mud mortar. The thickness of the mud joints varies in the present ruined buildings from 6″ as found at Santa Teresa, to 1″ at Oquitoa.

Adobe brick walls were necessarily heavy because of the poor bearing capacity of the material. The minimum thickness, as a rule, was about 3′. The early adobe walls were finished inside and out with a thin, hard adobe mud plaster and were given a heavy coat of whitewash.

Mud plaster offered but a temporary protection to the adobe, so a type of cement mortar was developed to be applied on the exterior walls. The best protection for the adobe was given when burned bricks became available. These harder bricks were used as a facing carried up the exterior walls to the top of the parapet where a molded brick cornice was constructed. These walls were always finished with stucco and given a coat of whitewash.

At Caborca we found the most durable construction. The walls here are of cemented stone and brick masonry, the facing, both inside and out, being of burned brick. The walls, as usual, have been finished outside with stucco and inside with lime plaster.

The planning of the churches was necessarily influenced by the materials to be used in their construction. Where vigas were employed to support the roof, the nave was quite narrow since timbers of any great length were not easily obtainable. Corbels were often introduced at the ends of the vigas to reduce the effective bearing span. This type of construction was used in the earlier and less pretentious structures.

Cocóspera offers an unusual type of roof and ceiling construction. Three brick arches springing from heavy brick piers span the nave. Mesquite beams are supported between these arches and are placed so as to form a rather flat barrel vault (see the reflected plan, and cross section, Figs. 4.I, 4.II). Small poles, placed closely together between the beams, are held in place by notches in the beams and form laths upon which a gypsum plaster is applied. A pitched roof is constructed of wood rafters spanned by small poles lashed to the rafters with rawhide. Burned clay roofing tiles laid in a cement mortar and supported on the small poles complete the roof. This is the only mission we visited in Sonora using the "mission" roofing tile!

Vault construction is used in the larger missions. An example of a barrel-vaulted ceiling is the one at San Ignacio. Here the nave is spanned by a simple brick vault springing from the adobe walls. Piers supporting a transverse arch are placed halfway down the nave probably with the idea of relieving the thrust from the heavy roof. Brick-faced adobe walls and relieving piers proved incapable of supporting the heavy ceiling, so we find the seemingly hurried construction of a massive buttress on either side of the nave, sufficient to relieve both the thrust from the vault and any doubts the builders might have had that the building would stand. A more successful barrel-vaulted construction we noted at Pitiquito (see Fig. 11.II); the use of barrel-vaulted as well as groin-vaulted ceilings is common in the minor rooms of other missions.

Domes are characteristic of the more pretentious churches. They are of several types, always constructed of a single shell of brick. The dome over the crossing is usually built upon an octagonal drum rising from pendentives. Window openings are placed in the drums. Caborca [then exposed by flood damage] offers splendid opportunities to study several varieties of dome construction, ranging from the very flat type to the hemispherical type. The architects of the missions were usually the padres themselves, who as a rule, conceived the work and directed the Indians in the erection of the buildings. In the case of Caborca and San Xavier del Bac, it is evident that trained architects were employed, and probably the same architect in both cases, since features throughout these two churches are so similar.

Although architecture did not constitute part of the padres' training,[13] a love for—and the remembrance of—familiar edifices in Europe and New Spain was carried with them to the remote mission outposts. Designing in the recollected fashion,[14] they erected the finest structures circumstances would permit. The primitive qualities of a pioneer country are interwoven with a conscious expression of the styles of the native land. The results constitute an architecture that is frank, simple, unrestrained, but alas, fast-fading under the hand of time.

DEVELOPMENT OF MISSION ARCHITECTURE: A "HANDBOOK" SUMMARY

For a proper study of mission architecture in the Southwest, one must necessarily turn to Mexico. Here the architecture is fashioned after that of the mother country, Spain, although all the architectural features of the Mexican churches are not directly traceable to Europe. It is necessary, however, first to consider the architecture of Spain and briefly to trace its development into the style which was later transplanted in Mexico.[15]

From early times the Iberian Peninsula had been under the domination of conquering peoples from the East—first by the Romans, then the Visigoths and in turn by the Moors, who were finally subjugated by joined forces from the north. The influence of these various peoples combined to give Spain a cosmopolitan architecture not found in other European countries.

Roman culture and influences form the basis upon which the Spanish civilization was built. Excellent builders, the Romans contributed the arch-and-pier systems of construction, the use of cemented-masonry walls, and the classic details and decoration. The Visigoths had little to contribute toward architecture.

The Moors, who dominated the country for almost eight hundred years, had a particularly far-reaching influence upon the arts and architecture. More decorators than constructors, their buildings were profusely ornamented, with little thought given to expressing structural elements. Decorations were lavishly used in the interiors, but the exterior walls were left plain except around the entrance and window openings. The use of stucco wall finishes was common with the Moors; also, they introduced domes and arches of Byzantine influence, with decorative motifs derived from the Persians and Syrians.

With the Christian victories in the north of Spain, Romanesque architecture was introduced from France, but later gave way to the Gothic style. Thus two great styles in the north flourished while the Moorish style continued in the south.

Architecture received a new impetus after Spanish victories over the Moors. Gothic structures under Moorish influences developed into the Gothic-Mooresque, a fanciful and florid style retaining something of the structural balance of the Gothic. The discovery of the New World and the final overthrow of the Moors brought Spain into a dominant position. The Renaissance style was introduced during this prosperous period, and developed with the Gothic-Mooresque to produce a style known as the plateresque and characterized by broad surface decorations particularly about the door and window openings, elaborated pilasters, and broken pediments and entablatures. The plateresque style was followed closely by the baroque (a classic revival) and later by the Churrigueresque (from the architect, José Benito de Churriguera 1665–1725).

The baroque style dominated from the later sixteenth century and through the seventeenth century, while the eighteenth century enjoyed the dominance of both the baroque and the Churrigueresque. Both styles are characterized by the interruption of straight lines, breaking of entablatures and pediments, and the ornamentation of panels.

The baroque style is characterized by the use of restrained columns which may be twisted, or storied, while the panels are undecorated and the profiles preserve their regularity.

The Churrigueresque is characterized by: highly decorated pilasters; lines infinitesimally broken; all panels decorated; and sculpture used as an integral part of the structure. These two styles often merge into each other and frequently show the influence of other styles in varying degrees.

This briefly outlines the cosmopolitan architecture introduced into Mexico by the conquering Spaniards. The earliest Spanish buildings in Mexico faithfully followed the styles of the native land. The influence of the Aztec, however, soon became apparent in carrying on construction with Indian artisans; the early structures bear their impress.

As in the colonial work of other countries, the architecture in Mexico, while basically that of the mother country, took on an individual character suited to new conditions. This Spanish colonial style was organic in character and rich in detail. Strong contrasts between plain and decorated surfaces were manifest, ornamented portions being: the facade, side entrances, towers above the roof, and the domes. The design and execution of the ornament was often entrusted to native hands and consequently not too well-developed nor refined, but free from restraint.

Domes were an important feature of Mexican architecture. Built with a single shell, the domes were often covered with glazed tiles of blue, yellow, black, and gold, and surmounted by a lantern.

Vaulted ceilings were almost invariably used except in the earliest structures erected solely for defense. The stone or brick vaulting was plastered—either decorated or plain. The prevailing color was white—the older decoration in bands, and centerpieces painted in dull reds, blues, and yellows, with an abundance of black used for outlining.

Spanish colonial in Mexico followed the change of style which took place in Spain, the plateresque, the baroque, and the Churrigueresque each holding forth but lagging in time behind the development of these styles in Spain.

While the prosperity of the new country was expressed in these magnificent monuments, the churches established to the north received little official attention. The padres in charge at the Sonoran missions managed to express in a few of the churches something of the splendor of these elaborate structures, as at Caborca, Cocóspera, and Tubutama. These churches *might* be called a provincial variety of the Spanish colonial of Mexico.

The main architectural features of the important Franciscan mission churches in Sonora may be listed as follows:

1. Solid, massive walls and buttresses.
2. Arcaded corridors, arches supported on piers, as at Caborca and Pitiquito.
3. Decorated area about the entrance, fantastic pedimented gables, as at Tubutama, Caborca, Cocóspera, and Oquitoa.
4. Belfries.
   (a) Two-storied towers, as at San Ignacio, Magdalena, Caborca, and Tubutama.
   (b) Single-story tower, as at Cocóspera.
   (c) Wall type, as at Oquitoa, and Atil (now destroyed).

5. Domes, as at San Ignacio, Magdalena, Pitiquito, Caborca, and Tubutama.
6. Roofs.
   (a) Barrel-vault, as at San Ignacio, and Pitiquito.
   (b) Flat-dome, as at Caborca, and Tubutama.
   (c) Flat (wood beams) as at Oquitoa.
7. Large areas of undecorated wall surface as at all missions.
8. Patio or partially enclosed garden area, as traceable at Caborca, Pitiquito, Cocóspera, and San Ignacio.

Solid, massive walls are characteristic of all the mission structures. This feature results from the necessity of building heavy walls of adobe for strength, stability, defense, and from the desire to create austere and noble edifices. Buttresses were introduced in many of the churches to strengthen the long, high walls and to react against the thrust from vaulted roofs and domes above.

Arcades are directly traceable to Spain. In the homeland the series of arches are usually supported on columns. In the Sonoran missions, the limitations of adobe, small stones, as well as the lack of skilled workmen dictated the use of simple, square piers in place of columns.

The decorated area about the entrance is, for the most part, the only elaboration displayed on the exterior of the missions. This elaboration is expressed in varying degrees, from the boldly conceived motif framing the entrance doors at San Ignacio, to the broader treatment of the whole area between the two towers on the facade of Caborca. The fantastic and pedimented gables reflect this same feature, which is common on the more elaborate churches in the south.

The bell towers in Sonora missions are usually two stories, with circular-headed openings piercing the walls in which the bells are hung. The towers are plain, surmounted by a dome, and crowned with a lantern. The lower floor of the tower at the church roof level is either of wood, as at Ignacio, or of masonry supported by a vault, as at Caborca. One example of a single-story bell tower, at Cocóspera, is constructed similar to the two-storied towers. A simpler form of belfry is the wall type [*espadaña*] which is merely a continuation of the wall above the roof, having arched openings in which the bells are hung, as at Oquitoa (see below, Fig. 7.2).

Domes are a characteristic feature of the churches in Sonora. They lend something of the Mediterranean atmosphere to many Mexican towns. The domes are generally constructed upon an octagonal drum which is pierced with small window openings to allow light to enter. At Pitiquito the drum

is not used, the dome here being supported directly on pendentives. Domes are usually placed over the crossing, but the dome at San Ignacio rises over the sanctuary. The shape of the dome generally is hemispherical, but an egg-shaped dome is used in Pitiquito. The interiors of the domes and drums were often painted with crude but highly interesting designs by native artisans. Tubutama still retains these decorative paintings now somewhat faded (see Figs. 13.II and 13.III).[16] Domes with tile-surfaced exteriors were out of the question in Sonora; the builders were content to whitewash them although at San Xavier the dome was painted to imitate tile.[17]

Barrel-vault and flat-dome roofs are common in the more pretentious mission churches. A brick interior cornice or molding is placed at or below the spring line of the vault or dome; exterior parapet walls of brick, finished with a molded brick cornice, carry above the roof in every case. Flat roofs are used in the simpler structures, wood beams or vigas supporting this type of roof. Carved wood corbels often are of Indian workmanship. Under the choir loft at Cocóspera, however, the carved wood corbels had been given a coat of plaster (see Fig. 4.8), but this practice was unusual. Simple brick parapet walls with a brick cornice were also used with the flat roof.

A common feature of all the Sonoran missions is the large areas of undecorated wall surface. This characteristic, of Moorish-Spanish ances-

FIGURE 1.5. San José de Tumacácori in 1864 (J. Ross Browne).

try, proved to be extremely practical in mission construction for Sonora because of the dependence on unskilled workmen. Any exterior elaboration was confined to decoration about the entrance and tends to illustrate [or coincide with] influence from the mother country.

Another Spanish element frequently used is the traditional patio or enclosed area which was so well adapted to the mission layout, if one considers the circumstances under which the churches operated. This courtyard feature was formed by the outlying buildings, walls, and arcades adjoining the church. We found many examples partially intact, or at least traceable, at Caborca, Pitiquito, San Ignacio, and Cocóspera.

The interior character of the missions varies from a severely plain treatment to a highly ornate and colorful design. The interiors of most churches have been whitewashed; much of the original colorful decorations consequently were covered over.[18] Tubutama offers most in the way of elaborate plaster decoration and retains many of the early colorful designs painted by the neophytes. Cocóspera, too, is colorful with finely executed painted designs, but in contrast, the plaster decorations tend more toward crudeness in execution. San Ignacio's baptistry still holds the stencil-like painted ornament so characteristic of the painted decoration in Sonora (see Figs. 3.VI and 3.VII).

Thus, we see that the Sonora missions more closely reflect the spirit of the Spanish colonial architecture developed in Mexico than any other string of missions established in the north [excepting, of course, Texas]. They, however, display the massive and primitive features which are justly and worthily expressed in an outpost of a new civilization.[19]

SCOFIELD DELONG AND LEFFLER B. MILLER

CHAPTER TWO

The Missions of Sonora and Arizona

Although the chain of missions[1] established by Father Francisco Eusebio Kino is the one with which we are directly concerned, it may be well to mention that actual missionary work in Sonora proper began about 1614 when Father Pedro Méndez, SJ, and a companion visited the Mayo Indians [in southern Sonora], and began to administer to them.

By 1636 the missionary frontier of Sonora was pushed up the Sonora valley, and a mission was founded in the vicinity of Ures. Father Bartolomé Castaños, SJ, was the first resident missionary (Ewing 1934, 22–23).[2]

The Jesuits were the first in this field, but in 1640 or 1641 Governor Luís Cestin de Cañas supplanted Captain Pedro de Perea as the governor of Sinaloa and almost immediately quarrels arose between the two concerning the limits of the respective territories they were to govern. Captain Perea was given jurisdiction over the territory north of the Yaqui River, which he named Nueva Andalucía and which was later known as the province of Sonora. He established his capital at San Juan Bautista.[3] Perea was unable to get along with the Jesuits in his territory, and he attempted to replace them with Franciscans, especially in the Sonora valley. Here for a short time five Franciscans under Superior Juan Suárez were scattered in the country claimed by Jesuits.

Then the Franciscans and Jesuits clashed. The Jesuit Visitor of Sonora, Pedro Pantoja, protested and sent Father Gerónimo de la Canal to the viceroy with a letter of complaint. Pending settlement of this dispute, Perea attempted to send Franciscan friars into the Pimería Alta (the territory in which we are interested), but the Indians proved hostile, and Perea was forced to abandon the project (Ewing 1934, 25).

Captain Perea died 4 October 1644, and shortly afterward the Franciscans were ordered out of the region by the authorities, leaving the Jesuits in undisputed possession of that missionary field. Thus, little by little, the Spanish frontier was pushed farther north into the Sonora valley; by the middle of the seventeenth century, missions were established as far north as Cucurpe and Arispe.

In March 1687 Father Kino arrived in Pimería Alta to begin his missionary labors, which were to continue without interruption for twenty-four years, during which time he founded the chain of missions with which we are concerned. He founded his first mission, that of Nuestra Señora de los Dolores, some 15 miles above Cucurpe, then the northernmost mission outpost in the valley of the Dolores River which joins that of San Miguel below the site of the mission some few miles. This first mission was on the site of the Indian village of Cósari (Kino 1919, 1: 51–52).

On 14 March 1687, Kino, in company with Father José de Aguilar, visited and founded San Ignacio de Cabórica, second mission in his series. Kino died at Magdalena at the house of Father Agustín Campos after celebrating the dedication mass of the new chapel at Magdalena. By this time, 1711, Magdalena had graduated from a *visita* of San Ignacio to a church more important than the latter place and was the residence of Father Campos.

The Problem of Father Kino's Burial Site (in 1935)

Although there has been some dispute over the actual resting place of Father Kino, all evidence [to date] seems to point rather definitely to the chapel in Magdalena as the place of entombment.

Dr. Bolton in his 1919 edition of *Kino's Memoir* (84), states: "His remains are now resting in San Ignacio, another of his establishments." However, Dr. Bolton has assured me that since that was written, he has other evidence which points to Magdalena as the resting place of this great pioneer missionary.[4] Lockwood (1934a, 41), states: "The greatest and undying distinction of Santa María Magdalena is that Father Kino, on 15 March 1711, died there in the house of Father Campos and was buried in the chapel of San Francisco Xavier." All local tradition in Magdalena certainly upholds the latter theory. Many efforts have been made to find Kino's tomb by interested residents of that city, especially Don Serapio Dávila. In 1930, he excavated in front of the present church—which was constructed and possibly finished in 1832—seeking the tomb.[5] Sr. Dávila has collected the reminiscences of many old men and women who remembered the ruins of Kino's church, the one he dedicated when stricken in 1711.

The building was apparently in a fair state of preservation in 1864 when J. Ross Browne visited Sonora and incorporated his impressions, verbally and pictorially in his *Adventures in the Apache Country* (1869). His view of Magdalena (Fig. 2.1) shows the old chapel and the newer church in the same relative positions indicated by the foundation walls of the ancient *capilla* visible today in the street and the imposing cathedral finished in 1832.

According to Sr. Dávila, the remnant of the bell tower and other portions of the older structure were torn down in 1882 and the stones used in paving the streets and sidewalks of Magdalena. This effacement of the old ruin occurred about the time the railroad was built. Attached is a rude sketch plan (Fig. 2.2), indicating the trenches dug by Dávila and the supposed location of the chapel in which Kino was buried. According to all observations by Dávila, the tomb must be under the site of the present *Casa Municipal*. Since the front of the old capilla fronted east-northeast, the altar at the side of which Kino was probably interred would be under the southwest end of the municipal building.[6]

FIGURE 2.1. Magdalena, new church and old chapel in 1864 (J. Ross Browne).

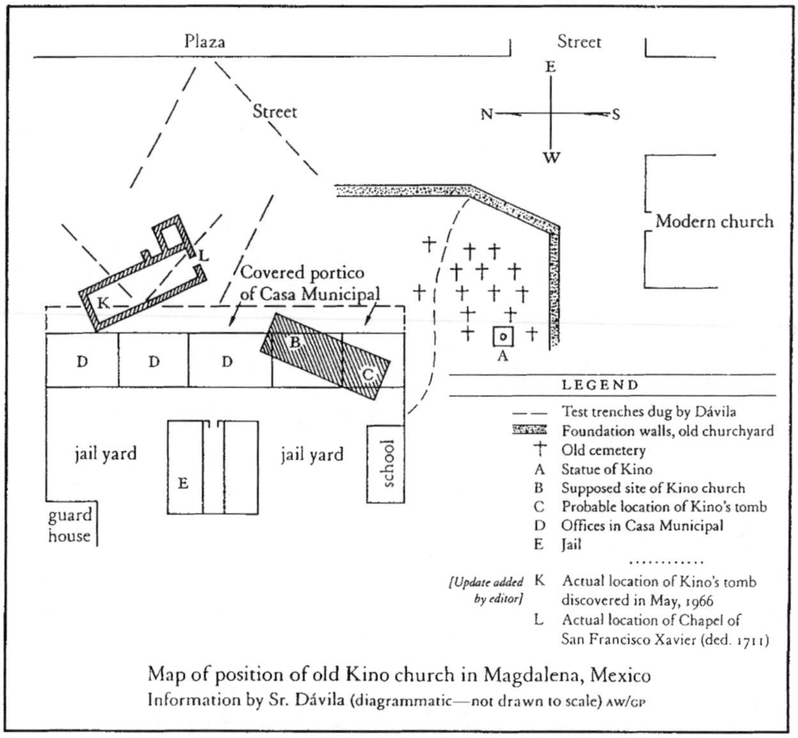

Plaza Street

Street

Covered portico
of Casa Municipal

Modern church

LEGEND
— — Test trenches dug by Dávila
░░░ Foundation walls, old churchyard
† Old cemetery
A Statue of Kino
B Supposed site of Kino church
C Probable location of Kino's tomb
D Offices in Casa Municipal
E Jail
....
[Update added K Actual location of Kino's tomb
by editor] discovered in May, 1966
L Actual location of Chapel of
San Francisco Xavier (ded. 1711)

Map of position of old Kino church in Magdalena, Mexico
Information by Sr. Dávila (diagrammatic—not drawn to scale) AW/GP

FIGURE 2.2. Magdalena, author's sketch plan of test trenches dug by Sr. Dávila, ca. 1928–30, in search of Kino's tomb. The actual location (K) is based on a corrected site plan (Polzer 1982, 62). (Woodward/Pickens)

The Missions After Kino

After Kino's death his work continued to be carried on by the Jesuits for more than half a century. In 1751–52 the great Pima revolt occurred which brought death and destruction to the missions. In 1767, according to Englehardt, the Masonic government of Spain brought about the expulsion of the Jesuits. Even prior to this time, however, the Indians at the missions had begun to show less inclination for priestly control. The unrest in the Pimería Alta continued to be reflected in the actions of the neophytes.

In 1767 the guardian of the Franciscan missionary college of Santa Cruz at Querétaro, under orders of the Viceroy La Croix, selected fourteen missionaries to proceed from Jalisco into the area from which the Jesuits had been expelled. These men assembled at the college chapel for a final mass and blessing before setting out 5 August 1767, on their northward journey. Some of these men were destined for Baja California; others were distributed among the missions of Pimería Baja and Pimería Alta.[7]

In 1768 the Franciscans of Querétaro accepted the missions of Pimería Alta in which we are most interested:

San Ignacio with the mission stations—*Santa María Magdalena* and *San José de los Hímeris*—was first occupied by Fr. Diego García, 1768–72.

[*Nuestra Señora del Pilar y Santiago de Cocóspera*. A fourth church may have been standing when Franciscan Francisco Roche took over in November 1768, after the destruction of Mission Suamca by the Apaches.][8]

San Pedro y San Pablo de Tubutama with the visita *Santa Teresa* was put under the charge of Mission President Father Buena in 1768.

San Francisco de Atil with the pueblo of *San Antonio Oquitoa* as a visita, besides two other stations near the presidio of Altar, was in the care of Fr. José Soler in 1768. At that time there was said to be no church at Oquitoa, and the one at Atil was a small and poor structure.

La Purísima Concepción de Caborca with *San Antonio Pitiqui* and *Nuestra Señora del Pópulo* or *San Juan de Bísanig* was given over to Fr. Juan Díaz, 1768–73. There was neither church nor house for the priest at Pitiqui.

Los Santos Angeles de Guevavi with three visitas: *San José de Tumacácori, San Cayetano de Calabazas*, and *San Ignacio de Sonoitac* came under the direction of Fr. Juan Gil de Bernabé in 1768. There was no church at Calabazas, and the others were described as poor. At Tumacácori there were some adobe houses and walls for defense.

San Xavier del Bac with the visita or presidio of *San José de Tucsón* became the residence of Fr. Francisco Garcés in 1768.

In 1772 Fr. Antonio Reyes, OFM, one of the Sonora missionaries then in the city of Mexico, compiled a report on the condition of the missions in both Pimerías. The entire district was then under the jurisdiction of the Bishop of Durango (see Reyes, "Report of 1772").[9] I shall not include the descriptions of the various establishments as given by Reyes at this time. Mention of the conditions of the missions will be given in their proper places. On the whole, however, the documentary sources are somewhat disappointing. No doubt there are many accounts which may give us more detailed information concerning the actual construction of these mission establishments, but so far they have not been given publicity.

FIGURE 3.1. Church from the southeast.

CHAPTER THREE

San Ignacio de Cabórica

Although this is the second of the Kino Missions, it was the first church visited by the National Park Service party. We arrived at Magdalena in the afternoon of 16 October and proceeded to San Ignacio the same afternoon.

San Ignacio de Cabórica is situated on the east bank of the Magdalena River, 9 miles north of Magdalena (see Fig. 1.2, above). To reach this mission from the main highway one turns off on a side road [at Tacicuri] about 6.7 miles north of Magdalena, taking the road that veers northwest for about 2 miles farther. The church looms up from a distance and affords a very pretty picture (Fig. 3.1). As with all of the churches, the location was chosen with an eye for fertile fields and a center of Indian population. At the time of our visit Sra. Leonor R. de Díaz, a fine-looking Mexican woman who owns a small store in the villa of San Ignacio, was custodian of the church. We arrived rather late in the afternoon and had no opportunity to do actual work—other than make a brief survey of the grounds.

On the morning of the seventeenth we arrived at 9:30, and after presenting our credentials to Sr. Hilario G. Nuñez, the *comandante de policía*, and obtaining the services of Sra. Díaz, we began active work. It must be remembered that in practically all cases the churches visited do not represent the structures actually built by Kino and his workers.

In June 1699 Kino was at San Ignacio, but at that time no elaborate church structure existed. Church services were held in the house of the priest for, as Kino remarked when, at vespers, he received a letter at this place, "I read it at the altar of our Father San Ygnacio (which is in the hall, because there is no church as yet), for in it was the lighted candle, and as I received the letter in question after nightfall" (Bolton 1919, 1: 201).

Apparently, this priest's house had been rebuilt after 1695, for in May of that year the Indians raided the missions of San Ignacio, San José de los Hímeris (the Imuris of today), Santa María Magdalena, and La Concepción de Caborca and burned the "houses or chapels."

Oddly enough, Kino does not mention any details of church or house construction at San Ignacio. Indeed, with but one or two exceptions (Dolores and Cocóspera), Kino is strangely silent on the subject of the actual building of his missions. It may be that the mundane problems of house and church construction were so prosaic and taken for granted that the eminent pioneer missionary did not consider the details worthwhile.

To those of us interested in reconstructing the physical aspects of the past, in making those places wherein the pioneers labored, lived, and died relive in all their glory, the memoirs of Kino and the Franciscans who succeeded the Jesuits in that field are relatively useless.[1]

As a matter of fact, the church, although it was the largest building at any one site, was not the mission proper. Too often we are likely to see the church that remains as the main feature of the mission. Physically, of course, it dominated the scene, and naturally, it was the spiritual heart of the mission, but in the outlying buildings surrounding the chapel pulsed the lifeblood of the station.

Usually the church had a *convento* or priest's quarters, kitchen, store rooms, etc., attached to it in the form of a square with a patio in the center (Fig. 3.2). At times, attached to this headquarters unit, if we may so term it, were the rooms occupied by the native major domo—keeper of the granaries, etc.—and nearby were the rows of smaller structures in which the more devoted neophytes lived. Generally, most of the converts lived nearby, sometimes in adobe houses, more often in the less substantial and more primitive wattle-and-daub or thatched shacks. Then there was the array of blacksmith shops, loom rooms, milling rooms, store rooms for agricultural implements, etc. The number of shops and living quarters depended upon the number of neophytes and their ability or willingness to perform the tasks allotted to them, and likewise upon the ability of their priestly teachers.

So, at San Ignacio we find the church building as the now dominant feature of the landscape, but if we examine the terrain in the immediate vicinity we also note many interesting features. The church building in itself is rather simple. The interior is not elaborately decorated (Figs. 3.3 and 3.4). As with all the churches which were in any fair state of preser-

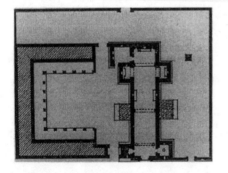

FIGURE 3.2. Conjectural site plan with *convento* (Duell, 1921).

FIGURE 3.3. Nave interior, *facing page*.

FIGURE 3.4. Side altar on the east wall of the nave.

vation, the altar furnishings, pictures, images, etc., had just recently been removed by order of the Federal Government in December 1934. In some cases—as at San Ignacio—the church furniture has been placed in one room of the church, usually the sacristy or the baptistry, and therewith placed under lock and key (the latter being held by local custodian), or else the door is sealed with one or two typed and stamped slips of paper which serve as official government seals.

Since it is not my intention to describe the architectural features of the building, I shall not attempt any such details, leaving them for Messrs. Miller and DeLong (see Figs. 3.I–3.VII).

We found a paucity of old furnishings in all the missions. Even before the closing of the buildings in 1934, many of the interesting items must have been carried away, either by the Mexicans themselves, or by tourists willing to pay the price, or in some instances stolen outright without payment.

In the baptistry was an unpainted wooden chest distinctly eighteenth-century in character, with the original, elaborate, iron lock escutcheon plate and hasp intact (Fig. 3.7). This chest was 42″ long, 20″ high, and 21-7/8″ [21-7/16″ on Woodward's drawing] wide. The corners were mortised together, and a simple interlocking circle decoration adorned the ends of the front of the box. In this chest were many fine old silk brocade and satin vestments, likewise of the mid-eighteenth century and possibly one or two that may have been used even earlier. Here also in the baptistry were a number of old images of San José who formerly occupied a niche of the east side of the nave, and opposite him was San Francisco, as well as several other saints. When John R. Bartlett visited San Ignacio in 1851, he mentioned the fact that two of the images were made over—"metamorphosed into saints"—from wooden statues of Chinese mandarin figures (Lockwood 1934a, 39) [from Bartlett 1854, 1: 420].

If such was the case, those two images have disappeared. All that we saw were old, original images, and not one that even remotely resembled Chinese workmanship. There were also a number of oil paintings of various sizes, some of fair workmanship in the baptistry, all pertaining to religious subjects.

In one corner stood a baptismal font of carved stone containing a copper basin and cover bearing a floral pattern in *repoussé* (Fig. 3.8). This font was 35″ high, the stone basin 27-1/2″ in diameter, while the copper lining, which was a separate piece and removable, was 20″ in diameter and 7″ deep. It was a handsome piece of copper work, the best we saw in any of the churches (see drawing, Fig. 3.V).

FIGURE 3.6. Detail of carved wooden doors (Duell, 1921).

FIGURE 3.5. Church portal *right,* with carved wooden doors.

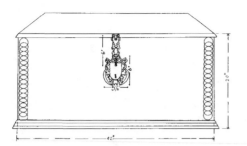

FIGURE 3.7. Eighteenth-century wooden chest in the baptistry (Woodward).

FIGURE 3.8. Baptismal font with ornamental copper cover.

In the baptistry proper were several places on the floor and the eastern and northern wall which had been recently repaired. Inquiry concerning these patches divulged the fact that in 1932 a man had approached Sra. Díaz representing himself as being a government employee sent out to repair certain cracks that had appeared in the baptistry walls. Accordingly she permitted him to carry in his tools, cement, and mixing vat, and then left him alone. However, his actions and secrecy about his work made her suspicious. She went to the church official in Magdalena and learned that no order for such repair work had been given. In the meantime, the "workman" returned the key to her and departed. She entered the sacristy and discovered that the man had been an imposter—merely another treasure seeker—and, instead of repairing the place, he had excavated large holes in the side of the room and at the foot of the baptismal font, seeking the ever-elusive gold and silver supposed to have been buried by the padres.[2]

The entire floor of the sacristy was replaced in 1914 after treasure hunters had torn it up. These same vandals also haunted the church at night and dug under the main altar. They worked at the right of the main altar, concealing their operations behind a sheet which they hung in front of them, and also moving the large statue of the Virgin to cover their movements. New adobe bricks replaced the ones which were dug up at that time.

Continuing on the theme of treasure hunters, it may be said here that in all the mission buildings and around the mounded remains surrounding the chapels, men seeking *tesoro* (treasure) have literally honeycombed the earth. One cannot walk around the environs of the main structures without skirting some of these holes, and in a few instances they are wide and deep.

In the sacristy of San Ignacio is a huge paneled chest of drawers, evidently made in the eighteenth century (Fig. 3.IV). This chest occupies the entire north side of the room, and although several of the drawers are missing and others are minus the iron handles and bottoms, in the majority of the compartments all of these are intact. A number of odds and ends of church furniture were stored in these drawers. Among the better items were two small, painted animal figures carved in wood (Fig. 3.9, sides). These were painted a dark brown—apparently the work of neophytes—and may well have dated to the latter part of the seventeenth or early decades of the eighteenth century.

Here also was an ebony and silver crucifix, apparently an altar piece (Fig. 3.10). This stood 29-1/2″ high, the cross arms had a spread of 18-1/4″.

FIGURE 3.9. Bronze crucifix with animal figures carved in wood.

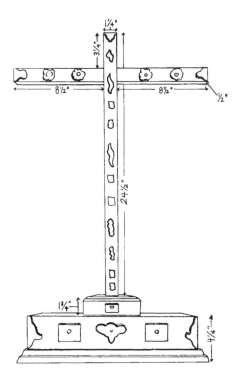

FIGURE 3.10. Ebony and silver crucifix (Woodward).

The upright of the cross was 1-1/4″ wide and 1/2″ thick. It was decorated from top to bottom with thin, silver ornaments in repoussé tacked to the wood.

In one of the drawers was a cast bronze crucifix, apparently meant to be carried at the end of a long staff in the processional. This was 21″ long and had a spread of 10-1/2″. It was a very neat piece of work (Fig. 3.9, center). Here too, were small wood and plaster images, parts of the decorations of the two side altars. These are in poor condition, some having arms, legs, and faces missing. Of course, the vandalism is laid to American tourists and probably with good reason.

The side altars which at one time were fine examples of eighteenth-century rococo work in plaster, gilt, and paint have been dismantled, and portions of them are scattered through the sacristy and the transepts. The wood is slowly disintegrating, and the various parts are broken and chipped.

Resting among the tarnished fragments of the side altar was a rusty U.S. Harpers Ferry rifle, model of 1831. It had formerly been a flintlock but was altered to percussion. The lock was missing, the nipple broken, and the ramrod gone. I learned that at one time there had been five or six old firearms in this church, including a flintlock or two, but these had been stolen. We heard that one of the latter type weapons was even then in possession of a Mexican living in town, but I did not get to see it.

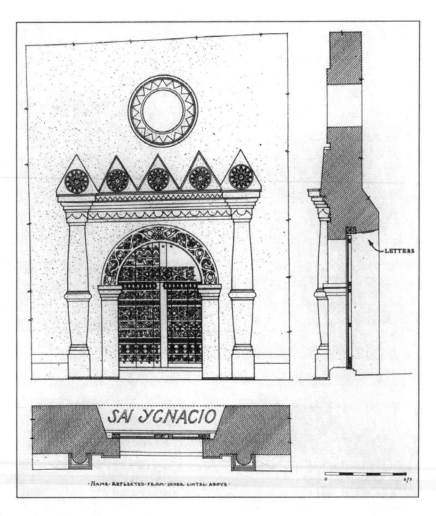

SAI YGNACIO

·NAME·REFLECTED·FROM·INNER·LINTAL·ABOVE·

FIGURE 3.11. Portal details showing molded letters above the wooden doors (Duell, 1921).

An interesting feature of decoration of this church is the wording "San Ygnacio" in large molded letters standing out in bold relief directly above the wooden door. These words cannot be seen from the outside, for they are on the underside of the lintel, inside the masonry arch of the main entrance (Fig. 3.11).

One old chair remains. This is of the type known as the *frailero* and was in general use not only in Sonora missions during the eighteenth century, but also in those of Alta California. A similar chair is in the Mission San Miguel in California; I believe another is in San Luis Rey, and yet another of the same type is in the Los Angeles Museum. Such chairs are entirely of wood, mortised and pegged together. A detailed sketch was made by Mr. Miller (Fig. 3.IV). The chair was used by the priest in the old confessional (Fig. 3.12) which stands in the nave of the church. This is probably contemporary with the chair. At least it gives every evidence of having been made at the same time (see also Fig. 3.III).

In the bell tower hang five bells. At one time eight bells hung there. Of the five I was able to read the inscriptions on the three largest ones. Those hanging in the north and south arches are cracked and useless. Judging by the workmanship they were cast locally. On the bell in the south arch is a crucifix in block pattern and the inscription in block letters:

BEATO IOBORIO AÑO DE MDCCCXXIII

On the bell in the north arch is the inscription in a peculiar combination of block and script letters:

AÑO DE 1813, EN JULIO XX D A CONCEUPCION

The bell hanging on the east side of the tower has the inscription:

YNANCIO D 1818

FIGURE 3.12. Old confessional with eighteenth-century chair.

It was not feasible to climb to the upper portion of the tower, the platform being rotten and no ladder available. From this tower one obtains a beautiful view of the valley to the south, west, and north. In the river lowlands immediately west of the mission are the lush growths of modern Mexican gardens planted on the very site of the old mission gardens and orchards. I was informed by Jesús Leyva, lessee of the ranch, who has lived here for the past forty-eight years, that formerly an adobe wall had enclosed the orchards; it extended up and down the river bed for a distance of 1.5 kilometers [nearly a mile].

In the environs of the garden may yet be seen the patriarch of all orange trees in the Magdalena valley (gray with age). It is 24″ in diameter at the base, approximately 20′ high, and has a spread of some 27′. Very likely this is one of the original trees planted by the padres; whether Jesuit or Franciscan it is very difficult to say. The tree continues to bear a profusion of extremely sour oranges.

Here also may be seen thick, untrimmed rows of *membrilla* (quince) and *granada* (pomegranate) trees heavy with fruit at the time of our visit (17 October). There are also stray fig trees lost in the tangled undergrowth, and farther down the valley there are said to be old pear trees which were also inside the adobe walls of the ancient *huerta*.

Along this rich bottom land the present occupant now raises his crops of sugar cane, chile peppers, beans, etc. They give him a rather slender income (about two hundred pesos a year according to current prices, which are very low). On this land the missionaries raised their foodstuffs: Here grew in profusion the squash, garlic, corn, beans, wheat, onions, and peppers that supplied the fathers and their faithful workers. This huerta was the garden of the mission proper. According to the system, the Indians who labored on a share plan drew their sustenance from the storehouses, while those who preferred to work their own fields were not entitled to a free distribution of such products.

Although we know from the records of Father Reyes that in 1772 San Ignacio had a church well furnished, with three altars, which corresponds to the structure standing today, and had the house of the padres adjoining the chapel, it would be difficult with this meager evidence to give any details of the establishment.[3]

At present, there are extensive ruins of an adobe quadrangle west of the church. Here without a doubt stood the residence of the fathers. The buildings were probably low one-story affairs, possibly higher in some instances, surrounding a patio (see Fig. 3.2, above). This collection of habitations, store rooms, work shops, kitchen, etc., was usually known as

FIGURE 3.14. Bell in east arch of tower.

FIGURE 3.13. Stair tower viewed across
the barrel-vaulted roof.

the *convento* or *dormitorio*. The Mexicans today use this term when speaking of such ruins. The church proper is usually referred to by the modern Mexicans as the *capilla* or *templo*. *Iglesia* is understood but not used as much as these other terms. It seems that *iglesia* refers to the modern churches. *Iglesia vieja* or *iglesia antigua* likewise brought results, but *capilla antigua* or *templo antigua* were better phrases when inquiring about the buildings.

It is impossible at the present time to obtain an adequate picture of the complete mission establishment and the various outlying structures or the periods in which they were built without some excavation properly conducted. North of the church were additional buildings, the ruins of which may yet be traced. Others have been obliterated by the settlers in the neighborhood.

The *camposanto*, or cemetery, was east of the church. A rubble wall, some 7' high and 21" thick, formerly enclosed this burial place. The east wall of the church formed one wall of the cemetery. In this wall were four or five oval niches in which skulls formerly reposed. This custom of decorating the cemetery enclosures with death's heads either by means of actual skulls or sculptured representations of them was not uncommon. The outer walls of the cemetery, like most of the outlying structural features, have tumbled down and are mere heaps of mounded rubble. One rather old and imposing tomb in which two or three bodies have been placed, had a small aperture near the ground at one end. This had been made recently, and through this opening the desiccated head of the body was visible, and fragments of the winding shroud had been drawn forth by curious children of the town.

In the center of the patio on the west side of the church a deep hole indicated the efforts of treasure hunters to locate some definite object. According to Sra. Díaz, an attempt had been made at that point to uncover the well which was supposed to have been dug there to supply the friars with drinking water.

Sra. Díaz asserted that her grandfather had lived at the mission when it was a going concern. Legend had it that one of the padres at that time kept the proceeds from the sale of cattle, sheep, horses, etc., in a large chest which he had under the bed. This box was said to be filled with golden *onzas* (a certain type of coin). One morning, according to the story, when her grandfather returned to the convento, after being away overnight at the direction of the priest, the chest was missing and the well had been filled to the brim with earth and rubble. The priest, too, had disappeared. This gave rise to the legend that the priest had buried the chest in the well, gone off to attend some other affairs, and failed to return. Since that time many have sought to uncover the well, but to date none has been successful.

Similarly, a story of a concealed tunnel entrance in the center of the nave of the chapel gives rise to other tales of tesoro. This tunnel, as with all tunnels (and nearly every mission was supposed to have one) is said to have gone off toward the river, to be used as an avenue of escape by the padres when the mission was attacked by the Apaches. Here in this tunnel are buried the gold and silver church vessels. Few Mexicans will admit believing the actual existence of the treasures or the tunnels, and laugh at the attempts of those who have dug fruitlessly for them, but will just as readily agree that there might be a chance that they really exist, and if given the opportunity would dig just as fervently for them.

Scattered around the outside of the church among the mounded walls and fallen stones are potsherds of plain reddish brown ware and some of the peculiar Trincheras ware.[4] The latter is common on all of the mission sites visited, save perhaps San Valentín where the pottery seems to be straight Pima-Papago.[5] I mention this fact in that it may give us a clue to the tribal identities of the neophytes who once lived there.

Early references speak of the Pima language being used by the Indians at San Ignacio, and since this mission was in Pima-Papago territory it is quite likely that people of these tribes were the servants at the mission. There are some puzzles, however, presented in the face of archaeological evidence at all of the sites which will need more careful field research before we can safely interpret the blanket tribal denominations of the early padres for this northern area of Sonora.

Evidence of activities of the mission, aside from farming, was found in the presence of two well-made tanning vats outside the west wall of the quadrangle. At present these vats, two of which are sufficiently exposed to be measured, are within a few feet of an irrigation ditch that winds along the gentle slope of the hill just above the river bed. The tanks are of different sizes and are constructed of cobble stones and lime mortar. The walls are 18″ thick, well plastered on the inside, and the largest of the two is 19′ long, 8′ wide, and from 5′ to 6′ deep. The smaller vat is in the best condition, although it has a small section out of one side. This vat is 5′ 10″ long, 26″ wide, and 33″ deep. No doubt further excavation on the hillside would expose other interesting features whereby a better idea of the activities of the mission could be learned.

Our work at the mission was aided by Sra. Díaz, the custodian, who not only unlocked the doors for us, but also gave us such information as

FIGURE 3.15. Church from the southwest.

she possessed concerning recent repairs to the roof, walls, and floor. Another resident of the pueblo who aided in moving objects about to be photographed, and who also helped in obtaining the inscription of the bells was Sr. Juan P. Buen, originally a native of Barcelona, who settled in this town several years ago. He was agreeable, a willing worker, and seemed to know the region in the vicinity of San Ignacio quite well. He would probably be valuable as a guide.

San Ignacio de Cabórica: Outline Description

ORIENTATION	South.
CONDITION OF CHURCH	Well preserved.
FOUNDATIONS	Rubble stone in cement.
FLOORS	Burned brick—semicircular, square 9″ x 9″, and rectangular 7″–8″ x 13″ and 2″ thick, laid in pattern.
WALLS	Adobe brick faced with burned brick. Molded brick cornice on parapet.
CEILINGS	Nave—barrel vault of brick. Sanctuary—brick dome. Baptistry—groined vault with plaster ornaments.
EXTERIOR	Finish—cement stucco, whitewashed. Bell tower—two stories; upper floor of wood beams and boards. Entrance pilasters at one time painted red and blue.
INTERIOR	Finish—lime plaster now whitewashed. Blue wainscot painted in nave; painted decorations still remain in baptistry (see Fig. 3.VI). Side altars of molded plaster over brick now whitewashed, were once highly decorated in red, blue, and gold.
DOORS	Main entrance doors of mesquite planks beautifully carved (see above, Figs. 3.5 and 3.6) in Renaissance design in low relief and ornamented with chased bronze studs. Doors swing on wood pins. Sacristy door of mesquite, paneled and with painted decorations (see Fig. 3.VII).
STAIRS	Circular mesquite stairs to roof.
OUTLYING BUILDINGS	Only mounded ruins remain to west of church.

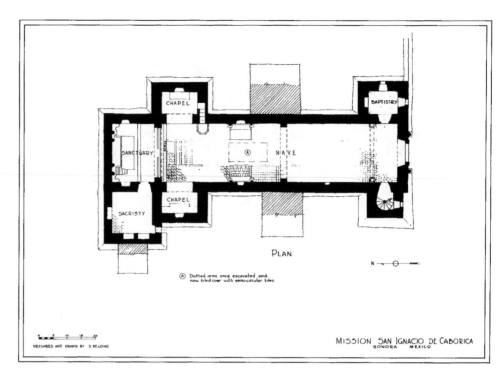

FIGURE 3.I. Plan.

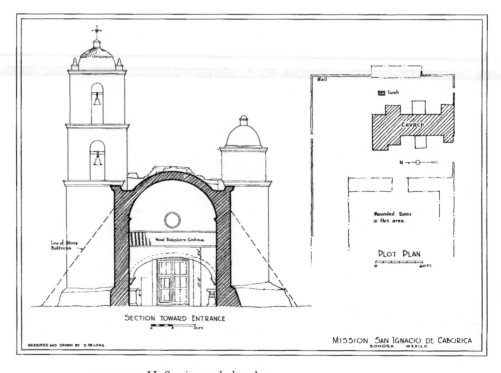

FIGURE 3.II. Section and plot plan.

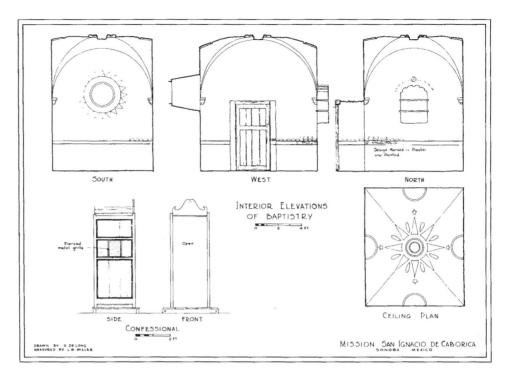

FIGURE 3.III. Interior elevations of baptistry and confessional.

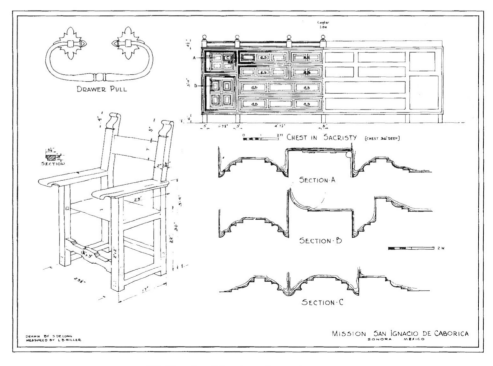

FIGURE 3.IV. Details of furniture in sacristy.

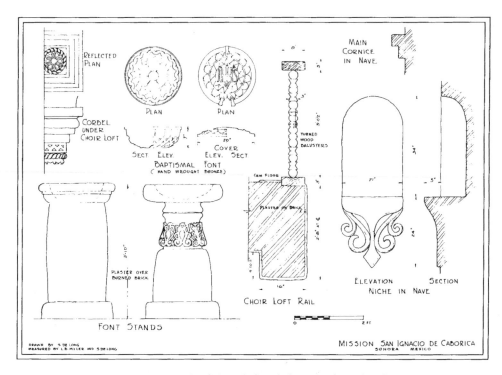

FIGURE 3.V. Details of choir-loft rail, font stands, and niche.

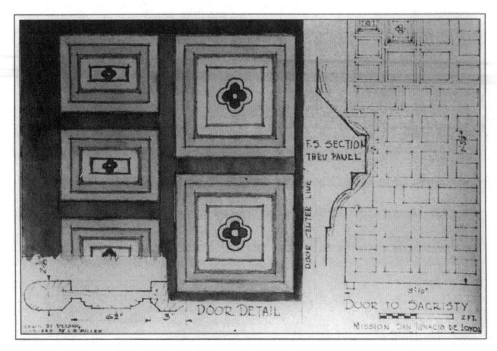

FIGURE 3.VI. Details of baptistry.

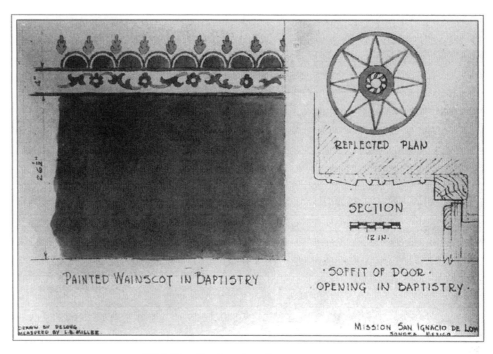

FIGURE 3.VII. Details of sacristy door.

CHAPTER FOUR

Nuestra Señora del Pilar y Santiago de Cocóspera

On 18 October we left Magdalena at 9:30 A.M. en route for Cocóspera. We arrived at the mission site at 12:20 P.M. and began work.

The road to Cocóspera leads through a wild and beautiful canyon through which flows a branch of the Magdalena River (Fig. 4.1). We crossed and recrossed this stream fifty-six times on the round trip between the mission and Magdalena.

To reach this mission from the latter town one drives north on the main highway to a crossroad marked EMPALME (junction), a short distance beyond the end of the cemetery fence on the outskirts of Imuris. This will be the first sign of this sort beyond the cemetery. Take the right-hand fork at this junction and continue northeast, keeping always on the best-traveled highway. This mission is 37 miles from Magdalena and is on the west side of the road as one proceeds up the valley (see map).

In 1864 J. Ross Browne visited Cocóspera and drew a sketch of the canyon through which the road passes for some distance. However, the pictures drawn by Browne are for the most part exaggerated to such a degree that they cannot be trusted for details. His Cocóspera canyon is drawn so as to give the wrong impression, and we could not recognize with any certainty the spot represented in his sketch.[1] Similarly, his views of the missions, Cocóspera (Fig. 4.2), Tumacácori, etc., are not only badly drawn but are inaccurate. The sketch of Tumacácori indicates a row of buildings, in line with the church facade, which never existed (see Fig. 1.5, above). In like manner, at Cocóspera his terrain is not correct, and details of the towers have been left out. [Compare Browne's sketch with a similar one (Fig. 4.3) by the French explorer, Alphonse Pinart, made in 1879.]

FIGURE 4.1. Río Cocóspera, one of 28 fords on the old road to mission from Imuris— 21 miles, 2 hours (L.C., Duell, 1952).

The mission site is on the crest of an old river terrace which slopes rather abruptly to the stream bed and at this point broadens out into a side valley; the current now flows against the far eastern side of the valley. Here in the fertile flats modern Mexican ranchers have their fields, and with very little imagination or exaggeration one may easily envision the landscape as it was when the mission was in its prime: with herds of cattle and sheep browsing in the pasture lands; with fields of corn, wheat, melons, squash, etc., growing luxuriantly in the rich loam of the flood plains; with the river marked by heavy verdant growth of cottonwood and willow.

Cocóspera, like the famed Topsy of *Uncle Tom's Cabin*—"just grew"! The date of the actual foundation of the church seems a bit hazy.[2] Kino was there in 1689, later in 1691, and probably many other times not mentioned.

In April 1697 Father Ruiz de Contreras became a resident priest. At that time, according to Kino (1919, 1: 166), the mission was equipped "with complete vestments or supplies for saying mass, good beginnings of a church and a house, partly furnished, five-hundred head of cattle, almost as many sheep and goats, two droves of mares, a drove of horses, oxen, crops, etc."

In March 1701 Kino went from Dolores to Cocóspera " . . . to cast a glance at my other two pueblos of Nuestra Señora de los Remedios and Cocóspera, because they were frontiers to the enemy, and to provide for their defense by means of some towers . . . " (Kino 1919, 1: 274).

FIGURE 4.2. 1864 view (J. Ross Browne).

FIGURE 4.3. 1879 view (Alphonse Pinart, Bancroft Library).

The master director of all these mission outposts was at Cocóspera again in April 1701, on his return south after visiting San Xavier del Bac. A church and house were being built in Cocóspera at this time by Kino's orders, and he paused here two days to supervise and direct the work (Kino 1919, 1: 292–93, n. 404).

During 1703 work on a large church building at Cocóspera was continued "zealously" in February, March, April, and part of May with the expectation of being able to have it finished and dedicated before the end of the year. The work was done mainly by Pima Indians imported from the neighborhood of San Xavier del Bac. The essential details of this construction are best told by Kino himself:[3]

In these months and the following, I ordered the necessary wood cut for the pine framework, sills, flooring, etc. I went to the interior and brought more than seven hundred dollars' worth of clothing, tools, and heavy ware and from other places I obtained more than three thousand dollars' worth, which shortly and with ease were paid for with the goods, provisions, and cattle of the three rich districts. I invited some men [Indians] from the frontier for the work on these buildings, and there came far and away more than I had asked for; and very especially, for entire months, the many inhabitants of the great new pueblo of San Francisco Xavier del Bac, which is sixty leagues distant to the north, worked and built on the three pueblos of this place and of my administration.

In this way many adobes were made in the two pueblos of Nuestra Señora de los Remedios and Santiago de Cocóspera; and high and strong walls were made for two large and good churches, with their two spacious chapels, which form transepts, with good and pleasing arches. The timbers were brought from the neighboring mountains and pineries, and the two good buildings were roofed, and provided with cupolas, small lanterns, etc. I managed almost all the year to go nearly every week through the three pueblos, looking after both spiritual and temporal things, and the rebuilding of the two above-mentioned new churches (Kino 1919, 1: 379).

The laborers on the church at Cocóspera were paid in corn, wheat, cattle, clothing, cloth of various sorts, blankets, etc., "which are the currency that best serves in these new lands for the laborers, master carpenters, constables, military commanders, captains, and fiscals" (Kino 1919, 1: 378).

In another place Kino refers to the wood used, saying, "The timbers for the frames and flooring, which are very good and almost all of pine called royal, were cut and brought from the neighboring hills, at a distance of seven or eight leagues" (Kino 1919, 2: 80).

A few additional [architectural] data concerning Cocóspera are included in Kino's relation:

OF THE MONTH OF JANUARY, 1704,
IN WHICH OCCURRED THE SOLEMN DEDICATION
OF TWO NEW AND CAPACIOUS CHURCHES

The churches of Nuestra Señora de los Remedios and Nuestra Señora del Pilar y Santiago de Cocóspera, as all who have seen them say, are among the best in all the provinces of Sonora, Sinaloa, Hiaqui and Chinipas. They both have transepts, formed by two good chapels, with their arches. One of the two chapels of Nuestra Señora de los Remedios is dedicated to our father San Ygnacio and the other to the glorious Apostle of the Indies, San Francisco Xavier; and of the two chapels of Cocóspera one is dedicated to Nuestra Señora de Loreto, and the other to San Francisco Xavier. *Each church has on the arches of the two chapels—which form the transept—a high cupola, and each cupola has in the middle and above a sightly lantern* [emphasis added] (Kino 1919, 2: 86).

The new year of 1704 was ushered in by cold, raw winds and a chilly weather; sickness prevailed. Yet in spite of all this a large concourse of Spanish *gente de razón*, visiting priests, and a host of natives from all parts of the Pimería Alta were at Cocóspera on 18, 19, and 20 January to participate in the dedication of the new church. Here were Yuma Indians from the far away Colorado River bearing gifts of the famous blue shells which led Kino to argue for a passage by land to California.[4] Here also were, "people from the nations of the Quiquimas, Cutganes, and Coanopas, etc., nations on the land route to California" (Kino 1919, 2: 87).

The dedication ceremonies "were performed by Father Rector Adamo Gilg, and other fathers, with all the ceremonies and benedictions which our Holy Mother Church commands, according to the holy Roman ritual." The choir from Remedios aided Father Gilg in the singing of the two principal masses. The dedication sermon was preached in Pima by Gilg (Kino 1919, 2: 86–87).

Such are the actual records by Kino of the building of a church at Cocóspera.

In July 1730 a Jesuit priest published an account, "Estado de la Provincia de Sonora" (*Documentos* 1853–57, 617–37). He mentions the church at Cocóspera as being in a ruined state.

On 25 February 1698 the Apaches, Sumas, Janos, and Hojomes attacked Cocóspera, "at a time when the pueblo was without men, for they had gone inland to barter maize; and although one of the enemy was left dead, they killed two Indian women, sacked the pueblo, burned it, the church, and also the house of the father, who was defended by the few natives who had remained. The enemy carried off some horses and all the small stock, and retired to the hills. A few from Cocóspera followed him, but when he saw them coming he ambushed them and killed nine of them" (Kino 1919, 1: 176). In this instance, Kino seems a bit inconsistent in his description of the attack. He states that "the pueblo was without men," then mentions the defense of the house of the father by "the few natives who had remained," and finally of the pursuit by a "few from Cocóspera" of whom nine were slain.

Apparently, at that time some sort of a church structure had been built at Cocóspera. However, on the afternoon of 22 April 1700 Kino again visited Cocóspera, "where we were received by one hundred and fifty natives who had just returned to settle this pueblo, and had just rebuilt and roofed a hall and a lodge for the father's house, with orders soon to roof the little church also, for three years before on 25 February 1697 (this should read 1698), the hostile Hojomes and Janos had sacked and burned this pueblo . . . " (Kino 1919, 1: 232–33; and for Bolton's correction of various dates, ibid., 1: 176, n. 211).

Forty-eight years later, in 1746, the mission was again burned. This was twenty-two years before the Franciscans took over the Jesuit churches. In 1768 the Apaches attacked Mission Santa María de Suamca, and Fr. Francisco Roche transferred the neophytes to Cocóspera, which at that time was a visita of Suamca (Englehardt 1899, 183). The following year, 1769, according to Bancroft (1884–89, 1: 689), Cocóspera suffered from an Indian attack.

It is difficult to determine just what the various writers meant by "burning" or "destruction" of a mission.[5] Judging by all evidence presented at the sites themselves, and our knowledge of Apache warfare, one finds it hard to conceive the destruction of any fair-sized building built either of adobe, burned brick, or rubble masonry. Likewise, it is difficult to interpret the records concerning repairs made to the buildings at different periods. Similarly, one is at a loss to decide how to interpret the statements about the erection of "new" churches. The details of such construction are so scant that the mere citing of work being done is relatively valueless when arriving at a decision regarding the types or numbers of structures that are supposed to have occupied one site. Cocóspera is no exception. There are a few scattered references in Kino's *Memoir* pertaining to the construction of the Jesuit church at this place.

On 16 February 1746, Indians burned the church, then a visita of Santa María Suamca ("Descripción geográfica natural y curiosa de la Provincia de Sonora, por un amigo del Servicio de Dios y del Rey nuestro señor, Año de 1746 . . . ," *Documentos* 1853–57, 607). Apparently, this was the original Kino church. We have no mention of its total destruction, nor is there evidence on the ground today that the fine structure described by Kino was ever demolished. One must regard the words "burned" and "destroyed" in connection with the missions as broad, descriptive phrases which are not all-inclusive in every literal sense of the word.

In the case of the earlier buildings—which in all likelihood were mere ramshackle huts built in the usual Indian style of either brush ramadas, or wattle-and-daub houses, or possibly small adobes—they could be destroyed very easily by Indian raiders. However, when one considers the later-type edifices, built substantially of adobe, rubble, or stone, with high walls over 40" thick and with sturdy stone buttresses, the Apache raiders (who came in with a swoop, lingered a few hours, and went out again) may have burned the roofs and destroyed the portable property of the church. But those Indians were not equipped to level such relatively huge buildings.

An examination of almost any of the mission sites today turns up proof of this assertion. *The enemies of the mission establishments were time and the elements, and the white settlers of the region* [emphasis added].

A roofless structure of adobe usually tends to disintegrate fairly quickly; on the other hand uncovered buildings may stand for years without appreciable deterioration, or at least no dissolution that may not be repaired quite readily with a few courses of new adobe and a roof of timber, brush, and earth. The ruins of missions in question, as well as those in California and elsewhere, are visible proof of this statement.[6] When treasure hunters and settlers desiring roof timbers, stones, door frames, floor tiles, etc., begin active operations in and around such buildings, then the destruction is very soon consummated.

At Cocóspera we made a survey of the buildings to determine some of these very points. Records stated that the buildings were "burned" in 1746. The present structure is in a poor state of preservation, but it is due to the activities of modern human vandals rather than Apache raiders. We know that the church and grounds were actively used until almost the middle of the nineteenth century—said to have been abandoned about 1845. Browne spoke of it being a "ruined old church." Owing to his inaccuracy in making sketches of such places,[7] it is difficult to determine how badly it was ruined.

Thirteen years before he [Browne] came to Cocóspera, John R. Bartlett stopped there, 30 September 1851. His description indicates it was in a fair state of preservation with wall and ceilings intact, decorations clear and complete, and even some altar furnishings left; towers and domes in good condition.

We found the church in a very ruinous state (Fig. 4.4). The outside is a facing of burned brick. In places, this veneer has pulled away from the inner wall, and by a careful examination of all breaks, inside and out, we made some rather interesting discoveries and deductions. It is presumed that the fine finish on the outside and the excellent gypsum plaster of the interior, the bell towers, and the buttresses, are of Franciscan origin.

Attached is a rough sketch indicating the main essentials of the ground plan of the mission establishment (Fig. 4.5). This is merely a sketch and is not drawn to scale [compare with DeLong's plot plan, Fig. 4.II]. Lack of time prevented extensive examination or detailed measurements of outlying buildings, wall, etc.

A Review of What Apparently Has Happened at Cocóspera

Kino's original church was of adobe. His two chapels, as mentioned, formed the transept. The interior finish was simply an adobe plaster, made smooth and hard and coated with a thin layer of whitewash upon which were applied designs in red, gray blue, and yellow. There were three simple windows in each side nearly 4' x 6'. These were guarded by

FIGURE 4.4. Facade, *facing page,* from southwest.

wooden gratings consisting of seven or nine wooden bars about 2″ square set transversely in vertical position. Heavy wooden shutters swung inward, thus protecting the church at those weak points. These windows were seemingly not centered opposite each other.

The Kino roof was probably flat except at the chapels, which were no doubt vaulted or domed. As with most of the early roofs, this one was probably composed of the pine vigas or beams, which in turn were covered with poles, grass, and earth. Such roofs need constant attention. The walls of this church were of adobe brick and were 42″ thick in front and some 53″ thick on the sides, and approximately 25′ high. The latter figure is problematical; the thickness of the walls is definitely known.

In 1746 the Apaches probably set fire to the roof and caused the abandonment of the mission for the time being. It seems doubtful that the Jesuits made repairs at Cocóspera after this. If so, they must have been very meager. That is, if we are to continue to base our belief in the Franciscan origin of the present structure.

About twenty-two years later, the Franciscans took over Cocóspera which was a visita of Santa María Suamca. Apparently, they built the present structure. However, this is what occurred *according to the building itself* [emphasis added]: The Franciscans, finding the heavy adobe shell of the Jesuit church in sound condition, simply built theirs *inside* and *outside* the original structure, adding to the side walls another 6″ of adobe and burned brick outside, and some 47″ of burned brick, adobe, and fine, hard, thick gypsum plaster to the interior (Figs. 4.6 and 4.7).[8]

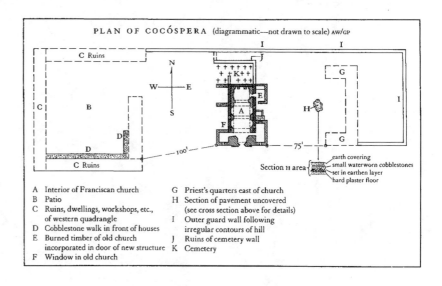

FIGURE 4.5. Site plan of the mission complex, no scale (Woodward/Pickens).

PLAN OF COCÓSPERA (diagrammatic—not drawn to scale) AW/GP

A   Interior of Franciscan church
B   Patio
C   Ruins, dwellings, workshops, etc., of western quadrangle
D   Cobblestone walk in front of houses
E   Burned timber of old church incorporated in door of new structure
F   Window in old church
G   Priest's quarters east of church
H   Section of pavement uncovered (see cross section above for details)
I   Outer guard wall following irregular contours of hill
J   Ruins of cemetery wall
K   Cemetery

FIGURE 4.6. Nave looking south toward entrance and ruins above.

They put a false front of burned brick and adobe on the church; added two bell towers; put in a barrel-vaulted roof [nave ceiling]; and completely changed the aspect of the building. They likewise added a tile roof [above the plaster ceiling vault] and probably installed the present choir loft (see DeLong's section drawing, Fig. 4.11).

They found the beams which had been charred by the fire of 1746 still sound, and instead of discarding these, they frugally saved and re-used them as sills and lintels in the new church. I found direct evidence of this in a door of the new structure on the east side (E, Fig. 4.5, above) which I pointed out to Messrs. DeLong and Miller. I also discovered the major evidence of the old church construction on the exterior of the west side, where part of a wall at the later building had sloughed away exposing a

complete window (F, Fig. 4.5, above) in the older structure which the Franciscan workmen had not bothered to fill when they put their veneer of adobe and burned brick inside the Jesuit walls.

To revert to the question of re-use of Jesuit timbers . . . opening off from the apse on the east side of the main altar is a door (E, Fig.4.5, above) which gave upon a series of rooms constructed along the outer wall of the Franciscan structure. Here I found a lintel, the *upper* side of which was charred, the under side being untouched. The Franciscans had scored the under side and then coated it with a fine, eggshell finish, gypsum plaster which they used throughout this church.

All exposed woodwork inside the building, even the nicely carved corbels (Fig. 4.8) of the beams upholding the choir loft, had been scored and covered. These beams were of mesquite and were of varying sizes, 9″ x 9″, 8″ x 6″, 7″ x 7″, etc., and they were socketed in mortar and burned tile. The floor of the loft was mortar 2″ thick, and at the sides near the walls was reinforced with fragments of curved roof tiles set in hard gypsum plaster. The carving of all the corbels was done with a narrow gauge or channeled chisel. The greater portion of the roof has collapsed (Fig. 4.9), except for a section over the choir loft and the dome over the main altar.

The latter portion of the church [around the sanctuary] (Fig. 4.10) bears the only remnants of a once-brilliant array of the decorative motifs of flowers, grapes, bananas, and huge vases in plaster relief filled with sprays of pomegranates. Vandals have chiseled one of the vases away, for what purpose it is difficult to imagine, unless they were searching for the eternal tesoro. Other fragments of decorated plaster relief bearing the faces of little *angelitos* have been deliberately cut out. This appears to be the murderous work of tourists, Americans probably—this breed seems to be the most destructive. Obscene pictures and the usual graffiti of foolish names have further destroyed the beauty of the primitive art.

It is not my intention, however, to linger on these details. Color sketches of some of the more pronounced features were made by Miller and Tovrea [unfortunately, these were not reproduced by NPS] while innumerable photographs of the interior, indicating all of the architectural and decorative details were made by George Grant (Fig. 4.11).

The old building swarmed with wasps. When we entered it just before noon these insects buzzed about in all directions and all of us were very wary of these miniature flying torpedoes. However, in the afternoon a breeze sprang up and all the wasps disappeared like magic into their nests in the adobe walls.

FIGURE 4.7. Side chapel, designed as niche within wall thickness.

FIGURE 4.8. Carved wooden corbels supporting the choir loft (WACC).

The floor is several feet deep with fallen roof and wall debris. Here and there treasure hunters have excavated in the crumbling mass of timbers, plaster, brick, and earth, but these were halfhearted attempts, and in no place did we find a patch of cleared floor. We did notice, however, that low down on the side of the west wall, small patches of crushed burned brick had been incorporated in the plaster finish as decorative motifs, similar to the effect achieved at Tumacacori on the inside of the two small transept rooms which are buried outside of the main structure at that place.[9]

As may be noticed in the sketch plan (Fig. 4.5, above), there was a [U-shaped] cluster of buildings (G) immediately east of the church (A). These formed some of the living quarters. The open space between the east wall of the church and these houses was partly paved with small waterworn cobblestones set on end (H). One odd thing about this floor or paving was that beneath the stones was a second, well-defined floor of hard-packed earth. It may be that the earthen layer marks the patio level in Jesuit times and the cobblestone paving may be a Franciscan innovation. At any rate, it invites speculation. No answer to this query could be obtained without excavation. Immediately east of the living quarters and emptying out upon the precipitous hillside was the well-preserved section of an open square drain. It was in line with the houses mentioned and could readily be followed by excavation [somehow, the drain does not show up on the author's sketch]. A similar drain, smaller in size, was one of the features uncovered during the excavations on the north side of the patio east of the church at Tumacacori.[10]

In the rear of the church, which faces south, was the camposanto (Fig. 4.12). Here were innumerable graves, many of fairly recent date. As with all these old sites, the Mexican inhabitants still prefer to inter their dead either in the old churches proper or in the cemetery near them. At one time a wall enclosed this cemetery with a gateway on the west side. However, this wall has been demolished; the burials have overflowed and are now spotted irregularly inside and outside the original walled enclosure.

As will be noted (Fig. 4.5, above) an outer guard wall (I), the foundations of which may yet be traced in good condition (in places), once surrounded the entire establishment. The buildings are fairly well guarded on the north, east, and south by rather steep banks. The defense wall followed the contours of this natural barrier. However, the west-northwest side was open to attack. Here the hilltop opens out into open rolling

FIGURE 4.9. Nave looking north toward main altar.

country covered with mesquite, and no doubt raiders probably attacked from that quarter.

Kino mentioned having gone to Cocóspera to provide for the defense of the place by means of some towers. Usually such towers—or *torreones* as they were commonly termed—were round, loopholed turrets, wherein the inhabitants of a mission or a town could rally for protection and make a last stand against the savage raiders. In a regular fort these bastions would be at diagonally opposite corners of a walled enclosure, but in Mexi-

FIGURE 4.10. Sanctuary with painted decorative motifs behind altar, *right*.

FIGURE 4.11. Details of painted and modeled decoration, *below*.

can towns the towers generally stood out alone. Although I inspected all portions of the area, I failed to notice any circular structures, or even the mounded remains of such. It may be possible that they did exist at one time and have since been obliterated, but it is difficult for one who has had archaeological training to concede the absolute effacement of such strongholds when lesser structures and useful buildings can easily be traced. Kino does not state that they were built, only that he went there to "cast a glance" at the two pueblos of Remedios and Cocóspera and "to provide for their defense by means of some towers" (Kino 1919, 1: 274).[11]

The terrain west of the church was occupied by a large plaza surrounded on four sides by rows of adobe buildings. Some of these are fairly recent in origin and were occupied until within about seventy years ago, or possibly less. This was no doubt the "pueblo" wherein dwelt Pima, Papago, and Yuma neophytes (I add Yuma because the baptismal records for 1822–36, signed by Fathers Francisco Solano García, Rafael Díaz, and José María Pérez Llera, in the manuscript collection of the Bancroft Library, indicate some Yuma Indians were present at Cocóspera in those years).

Here also dwelt the Spanish-Mexican residents. Fragments of blue and white, and lavender and white English porcelain—dating from about 1820–40, are found in abundance on the surface, thus corroborating "los libros de Bautismo y Entierros" as occupational evidence during that period.

To obtain an accurate ground plan without excavation is impossible. One interesting feature of this western group of buildings is the well-cobbled sidewalk (D, Fig. 4.5, above) which remains along the inner side of the southern and part of the eastern row of houses. This walk is about 6′ wide. Similar walks or pavings may be seen in all of the small Mexican communities of Sonora today.

I believe, however, that the houses which were the last to be occupied were reconstructed habitations, built on the foundations of earlier structures, and were in use until about sixty or seventy years ago. A Sr. Vásquez, *ranchero* in the neighborhood, stated that his father, now deceased, remembered when the mission buildings were in use. The usual debris of glass bottle fragments, bits of porcelain dishes, and scraps of iron work, indicative of an occupation for the period of 1870–80, were scattered around over a part of the area, mingling with the more ancient Indian pottery and Mexican glazed ware.

That this region yet remembers the Apache is quite evident in the tales told by the rancheros. Sr. Vásquez pointed out a tall, blue peak looming

FIGURE 4.12. Cemetery and rear (north) view of the church.

on the southern horizon, which he affirmed was the lookout used by Gerónimo and his warriors; and from their camps on this mountain the Indians spied on the valley below and made their sudden raids upon the little towns and ranches.

Now all is desolation at Cocóspera. The wasps are the only living things inhabiting the ruins. The site is wrapped in a thorny winding sheet of mesquite and cactus. In the side valley below are the fields and pastures of the modern rancheros. At the foot of the hill whereon the crumbling walls of Cocóspera stand is the ranch of the Proto brothers, who own this bit of historic ground.

We left Cocóspera with regret, knowing that here we had found a most interesting site, one which would yield more information if carefully studied,[12] yet our time was limited and we could not stay.

FIGURE 4.13. Ruins of church from southeast.

Nuestra Señora del Pilar y Santiago de Cocóspera: Outline Description

ORIENTATION	South.
CONDITION OF CHURCH	Roof fallen, towers mostly gone, walls still standing are fast crumbling.
FOUNDATIONS	Rubble stone laid with cement.
WALLS	Double walls showing one church constructed inside of an earlier structure. Old walls are of adobe. Later walls are of adobe and burned brick. Molded brick cornice on parapet capped with roof tiles. Stone-faced buttresses with stucco finish on each side of nave and at rear of church.
CEILINGS	Nave—flat, plaster barrel vault supported on transverse adobe ribs. Plaster is applied on saguaro ribs placed between mesquite beams bearing on these adobe ribs. [This unusual construction is explained in the reflected ceiling plan (Fig. 4.I), and in the cross section and detail (Fig. 4.II).] Sanctuary—brick barrel vault.
ROOF	Timber joists spanned by small poles lashed in place with rawhide and supporting mission roof tiles laid in cement (Fig. 4.II).
EXTERIOR	Finish—stucco on burned brick and adobe.
INTERIOR	Finish—exceptionally hard, thick gypsum plaster on walls and ceiling. Sanctuary walls and ceiling vivid with colorful paintings fairly well preserved. Choir loft—7″–8″ square mesquite floor beams and carved wood corbels finished with gypsum plaster.
STAIRS	Circular plan in east tower (see detail Fig. 4.III), mesquite steps to the roof, with the soffit and center column plastered.
OUTLYING BUILDINGS	Remains of a few adobe walls east of church with a paved area in front overgrown and covered with dirt and debris. A portion of the adobe, cemetery wall still stands, and foundations of guard wall on north and east of church are traceable. Large area west of church is enclosed by mounded ruins with a stone terrace [walk?, cf. D, Fig. 4.5, above] along the south side of this area (see plot plan, Fig. 4.II).

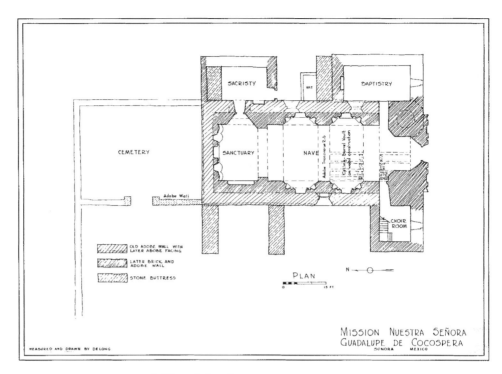

FIGURE 4.I. Plan of church.

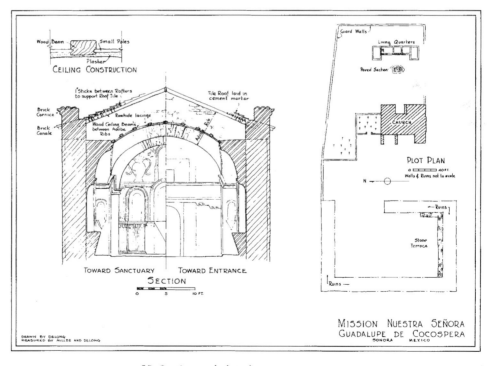

FIGURE 4.II. Section and plot plan.

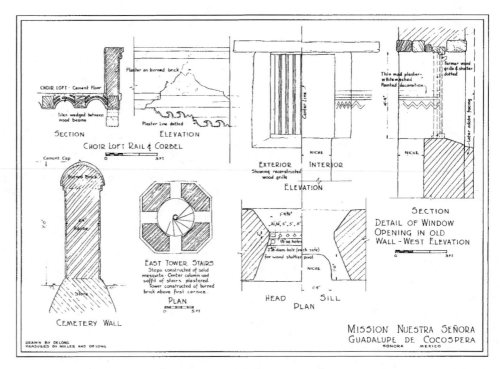

FIGURE 4.III. Details: Choir-loft rail and corbel, window opening in old wall, cemetery wall, and east tower stairs.

CHAPTER FIVE

Santa María Magdalena

On 19 October we decided to make a few notes at Magdalena. However, since the church here was the product of the nineteenth century we felt that it had not a definite place in our studies of Jesuit and Franciscan architecture (Fig. 5.1). Moreover, the building does not even stand upon the site of the older Jesuit church, as I have already noted (chap. 2, p. 19).

When we were in Magdalena all of the regularly inducted officials had fled the town fearing assassination. There was no presidente nor chief of police. Federal soldiers guarded the telegraph and post office and the Casa Municipal. At the latter place I presented our credentials and explained the purpose of our visit. After some hesitation, Sr. Pablo Flores, the temporary deputy and custodian of the keys to the church, opened the door and let us in.

According to Sr. Dávila this building was constructed in 1833.[1] The interior has been redecorated, probably early in the twentieth century. As with all the churches visited which were in usable condition, the altar furnishings, pictures, and statues had been removed and deposited in a side room, under lock and key and paper seal, by the Federal authorities.

Here in the church was kept the image of San Francisco Xavier, the statue beloved by Father Kino. Vested in rich garments, it formerly reclined at full length in a glass-encased box (Fig. 5.2). At Hermosillo we heard common gossip about the streets that the image had been burned. One informant stated that it had been incinerated in the boilers of the local brewery. This happened just last year (1934), probably shortly after the decree was issued to close the churches. In Magdalena, the cremation of the image was at first denied but later the same man who had made this

FIGURE 5.1. 1830s church near site of
Padre Kino's grave.

statement admitted that it actually had been destroyed. It is said that ex-
President Calles's son wears one of the fingers of this statue on his watch
chain.[2]

From the tower of this church we obtained a good view of the old
outlines of some of the walls of the original churchyard enclosure now in
the street in front of the present edifice.

Originally there was a facade on this church, but it fell of its own
weight. All in all this building is not as interesting from the viewpoints of

FIGURE 5.2. Reclining image of San Francisco Xavier (Thomas H. Naylor).

antiquity, architecture, or history as others we visited. Accordingly we spent but a short time at this place. There was somewhat of a tension felt in Magdalena, and for that reason too, we did not care to prolong our visit. Our guide who opened the door for us was plainly ill at ease and somewhat nervous over our presence.

When Dr. Russell[3] was in Magdalena last year (1934), the church had been converted into a public meeting place for the anti-religious group. Inside the church evidences of these meetings were before us in the form of large newspaper portraits of Zapata, Calles, et al.[4] pasted on the walls of the nave. On a side wall was a pencil sketch of a hammer and sickle and a Calvary cross overthrown. There were some chairs and a table which had been used by the local members of the agrarian group. However, dust was over everything, and it did not appear to have been used for some weeks. The large banner which had been so prominently displayed on the outside of the building was not in evidence.

For local traditions concerning the location of the ancient capilla, one should contact Don Serapio Dávila, storekeeper in Magdalena. He has gathered data from various old residents who remembered the old church when it was still standing. This I have noted above (see "Authors' Introductions," pp. 18–19) and in the sketch plan (see above, Fig. 2.2).

Santa María Magdalena: Outline Description

ORIENTATION	North.
CONDITION OF CHURCH	A modern [i.e., 1830–32] but not particularly interesting structure in good condition.
FOUNDATIONS	Cemented stone.
WALLS	Burned brick with molded brick cornice.
CEILINGS	Nave—flat domes between transverse brick ribs. Crossing—dome on octagonal drum.
EXTERIOR	Finish—stucco, whitewashed.
INTERIOR	Finish—whitewashed lime plaster. Main Altar—recent classic design. Side Altar—older and more interesting with gold and white columns.

CHAPTER SIX

Altar

[Site of a Former Presidio, Not a Mission][1]

Leaving Magdalena on the afternoon of 19 October, we proceeded to Altar making the trip in about three hours. Having a note of introduction to Pablo Chavarín from his brother in Magdalena, I asked for him at the Escobar home, which stands on the east side of the plaza. At the *casa* we found Hernández Escobar who, upon learning of our quest concerning ancient buildings, proceeded to inform us that there had been an ancient capilla in Altar which has now been entirely obliterated.

This was interesting news. We had no information concerning such a church. The various writers who have discussed the churches in Sonora have not mentioned a chapel in Altar, and the present building dates from 1846, the year in which it was commenced. It was completed in 1886 according to Alberto Escobar, brother of Hernández.

Furthermore, we were informed that Alberto had made a pencil sketch of the old building as well as a ground plan. These were produced and copied on film by George Grant (Figs. 6.1 and 6.2). As a precaution, a tracing of the original was also made.

At present the site of the old church—which was probably begun contemporary with the establishment of the presidio of Altar [1755][2] and used until the modern structure was put into operation in 1886—is occupied by a *cantina* operated by Sr. Chavarín, brother-in-law to the Escobars. When foundations for the cantina were dug, many human skeletons in the old cemetery were found and left in place. This camposanto is said to have been abandoned as a place of sepulture about 1850.

In appearance the old church was much the same as the mission of Atil near Santa Teresa. Probably this church was not administered as a mis-

sion, but was a presidial church, served by one of the padres from the nearby mission of Oquitoa [actually Atil].[3] It will be noted too, that an outside stairway led to the choir loft. This was a feature at Oquitoa. The bell gable on the roof was similar in appearance to that of Atil. The building was marked by the same simplicity of construction as those churches we found at Atil, Santa Teresa, and San Valentín.

According to Ewing (1934), the presidio of Altar was founded after the Pima revolt, probably about 1752–54. In a ground plan of the town[4] made between 1766 and 1768 by Joseph de Urrutia (Fig. 6.3), the old chapel (*Yglesia*) is shown standing on the site (c) ascribed to it by the Escobars. Furthermore, on the same plat are indicated the *Casa del Capitán* (B), and the *Cuerpo de Guardia* (A), as well as the *Patios de la Casa del Capitán* (F). These are: the Captain's house; guard's house; and the patio of the Captain's house.

We were informed that the Escobar house was the ancient headquarters of the first military commander at Altar, and that the patio in the rear of the house, filled with a riot of citrus, other trees and plants, and tall old palms rising skyward, was the garden *del comandante*, and that the small house on the northwest corner of the square adjoining the Escobar residence had been the guard house. This local tradition is corroborated by the Urrutia plan of the town. Copies of this same plan of Altar are to be found in the Arizona Pioneers' Historical Society, Tucson, and in the Bancroft Library, Berkeley, California. In the same collection [of copies] at Tucson is also a Urrutia plan of the old presidio of Tubac, Arizona.[5]

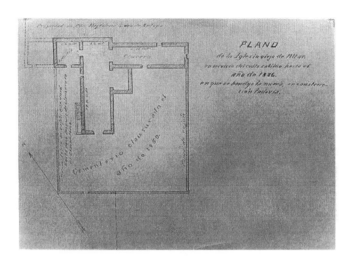

FIGURE 6.2. 1886 plan of the old church (Escobar).

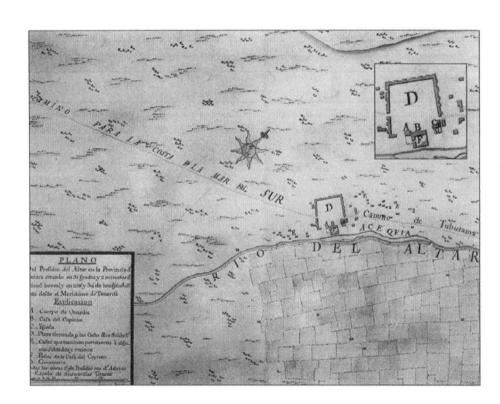

FIGURE 6.3. 1768 plan of presidio by Joseph de Urrutia (British Library, copy L.C.).

FIGURE 7.1. Exterior from the southwest
showing tombs in cemetery.

CHAPTER SEVEN

San Antonio de Oquitoa

We went from the town of Altar to the ranch of Mr. Roy Cutting about 5 miles east of town. Here we made our headquarters during our sojourn in and around the Altar valley.

Our next objective, the mission church of Oquitoa, we visited on 20 October. Here we have a Franciscan church of burned brick and adobe standing on a hill overlooking the sleepy little pueblo of Oquitoa. This mission was designated [by Reyes] as a visita of San Francisco de Atil in 1768,[1] when the Franciscans took over the missionary work in Sonora. However, no church was listed at that point nor was there any house for the priest. Hence, the present structure seemingly must date well after the beginning of the Franciscan occupation.[2]

At present it is a charming little church (Fig. 7.1). It faces south and in its heyday must have presented a lively scene. Aside from the chapel, there were a number of neophytes' houses. These were adobe structures which stood to the south directly in front of the church on the relatively smooth, slightly sloping top of a long point of land. Now these quarters are marked only by mounds of earth and potsherds.

Surrounding the church are many tombs. These are curiously elaborate affairs built in the form of small chapel-like cubicles, bearing miniature domes, lanterns, and crosses. From a distance the hilltop takes on the appearance of a small oriental city gleaming white in the sun; one almost expects to see the place swarming with inhabitants. Hanging on the crosses of the graves are wreaths of broken glass. These are manufactured by certain men in Oquitoa. The glass is obtained from old colored bottles. It is first burned until it cracks into small pieces. This friable glass is not jagged, and the peculiar crackled effect obtained in heating adds to the appearance of the funerary offerings making the *coronas*—as they are termed by the Mexicans—glisten in the sun like so many diadems of diamonds, rubies, and emeralds.

The church itself is very simple (see plan, Fig. 7.I), befitting in aspect that of a visita. The three-storied facade (Fig. 7.2) however is, or rather has been, somewhat ornate [i.e., more complex—a studied frontispiece—integrating within the wall plane: a simulated tower with espadaña (twin-arched belfry); pilasters; cornices; five niches; and the familiar curvilinear molding].[3] But time and the elements have played havoc with the stucco detail and painted designs, except for some still visible at the splayed portal.

In recent years the church has undergone repairs and reconstruction.[4] How much of this type of work has been carried on since it was first built is difficult to determine (Figs. 7.3 and 7.4). About 1920 the cane roof was renewed and one or two vigas (rafters) were replaced, but the remainder of the vigas and the corbels seem to be original. Also in 1920 the present choir loft was built. Two side windows were also cut in the church at the same time. In the baptistry is a baptismal font of hammered copper supported on a carved wooden stand. This was unique, since all the other baptismal fonts were of carved stone and copper (see the measured drawing, Fig. 7.II).

In this same room are also six oil paintings of the crucifixion; these are 31″ x 38″ and represent the following scenes: the Vía Dolorosa; placing the crown of thorns on Christ's forehead; the scourging of Christ; the crucifixion with the Roman soldier plunging the spear in Christ's body; the descent from the cross; and placing the body in the tomb. These are fairly well executed by Mexican artists, done sometime during the first three decades of the nineteenth century, judging by the costuming of one or two of the figures.

In the sacristy which adjoins the baptistry are four old rifles. One is a Springfield tapelock of 1855; two are Marlin and Remington single-shot rifles patented in 1870, and the fourth is a percussion-lock musket, made in Danzig, Germany [now Gdansk, Poland], which has been altered from flint to percussion lock. Other than three small bronze bells there was no item pertaining to the church rituals in either the baptistry or the sacristy.

We returned the key to the custodian, Ramón Figueroa, who lives in a small adobe hut southeast of the main part of Oquitoa. Here we saw one of the rawhide sacks known as *tanate* (Fig. 7.5). Such containers have been

FIGURE 7.2. Facade from the south, *facing page.*

FIGURE 7.5. *Tanate* or rawhide sack; such sacks, while not uncommon in Mexico, were used in California, Arizona, and New Mexico, and probably in Texas as well (Woodward).

FIGURE 7.3. Main altar in 1935.

manufactured in Mexico for several centuries and must have been in use at the time the northern part of Sonora was being colonized. Figueroa also had a small bowl of broken glass fragments prepared for corona making. However, he stated that he only prepared the glass, and the actual labor of making the wreaths was done by another man in the town.

A waterwheel in Oquitoa supplies the power for the flour mill. At times the same power turns the small ore-reducing mill. The present mill does not seem to be very old. Apparently, however, the town of Oquitoa has long been a milling center. During the 1860s two flour mills were located here; and from these establishments came the coarse, poorly-ground flour which supplied the U.S. Federal forces in Arizona, then stationed at Tucson, Tubac, etc.

FIGURE 7.4. Main altar in the 1920s
(George Boundey, WACC).

San Antonio de Oquitoa: Outline Description

ORIENTATION	South-southeast.
CONDITION OF CHURCH	Fairly well preserved.
FOUNDATIONS	Rubble stone in cement.
FLOORS	Brick, laid in herringbone pattern in nave. Square tiles in baptistry and sacristy.
WALLS	Adobe with burned-brick facing.
CEILINGS	Round and square ceiling beams throughout, spanned by cane and split saguaro ribs. Carved wood corbels under nave ceiling beams. Sanctuary ceiling about 3′ higher than nave ceiling.
EXTERIOR	Plaster over brick. Stone buttresses at rear.
INTERIOR	Finish—lime plaster whitewashed. Evidence of painted wainscots under whitewash.
DOORS	Flush-panel plank doors of mesquite.
CHOIR LOFT	New wood construction.
STAIRS	Outside brick stairs to choir loft.
BELFRY	Espadaña (wall type—integrated in design of facade).
OUTLYING BUILDINGS	Portions of adobe cemetery wall still standing adjoining west wall of church.

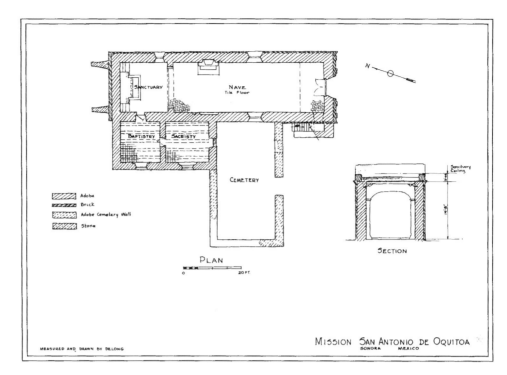

FIGURE 7.I. Plan and cross section.

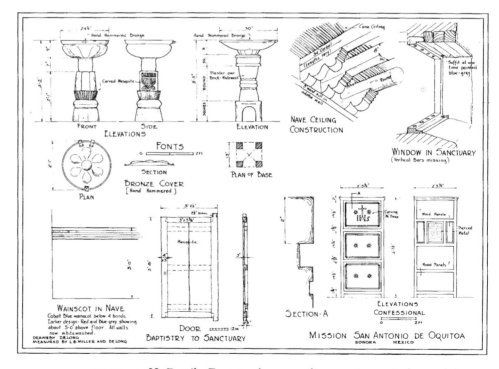

FIGURE 7.II. Details: Font stands, nave ceiling, sanctuary window and door,
wainscot in nave, and elevations of the confessional.

CHAPTER EIGHT

San Francisco de Atil

This mission of which Oquitoa was a visita is some 5 miles north of Oquitoa. It is mentioned as having a very small, poor church in 1768 when Fr. José Soler, the first Franciscan, came to take charge.[1]

We arrived at the town of Atil at 4:30 P.M., Sunday, 20 October 1935, for a cursory examination of this chapel. The church faces east [south-southeast according to DeLong's floor plan, Fig. 8.I] and is within the limits of the town. The old structure is now in a sorry state and within a few more years will be a formless mass of melted walls. The ruins of the ancient church stand alongside a more modern structure (Figs. 8.1 and 8.2).

The fallen walls prevented any accurate deductions, and the fact that the building has been patched and rebuilt in times past made the task of determining the physical aspect quite difficult.[2] An example of this rebuilding was evident in the ruins of the main altar. Originally, the interior of the chapel had been plastered with a thin coat of poor plaster, and the west end had been painted red. This red plaster had been scored into squares, and outline figures of fruit, birds, etc., were crudely scratched on this imitation tiled background. Later, the main altar of adobe bricks was built across the end of the church hiding this original decoration (Fig. 8.I).

It may be well to note at this time that in early-eighteenth-century buildings, and late-seventeenth-century edifices—in Sonora at least—the plaster was usually a thick, poor whitewash.

Included is a sketch of the ground plan of the church (Fig. 8.3). It is not drawn to scale and includes the ruins of the chapel and part of the priest's quarters. In modern times, the present occupants of the village have al-

FIGURE 8.1. Church in 1935.

tered the old church, walling up arches and making storerooms of some of the old living units.

Alongside the ancient chapel on the east stands the modern church. This is an uninteresting building, and since it had no part in our studies we did not examine it. I was informed that the old cemetery was in front and on the side of this later building; in other words, it would appear that the new church was built within the confines of the burial ground.

As may be noted in the sketch, the line of building formerly extended to the east and south of the old church. On the west side was a walled enclosure. This church originally had a bell gable which was reached by a series of steps on the west side. This gable stood until this last year or so. It has now entirely disappeared, and the bells are suspended in front of the modern church. These are fairly new bells, having been cast in 1903.

FIGURE 8.2. Church as it was in 1921
(Duell, AHS).

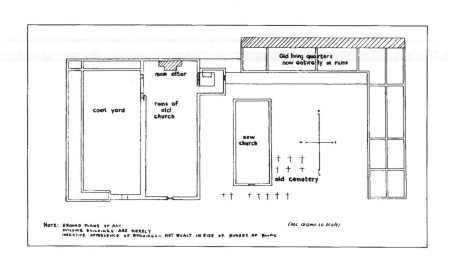

FIGURE 8.3. Mission site plan
(Woodward).

San Francisco de Atil: Outline Description

ORIENTATION	South-southeast.
CONDITION OF CHURCH	Ruined walls still stand approximately 15′ high.
WALLS	Adobe bricks with burned-brick facing.
ROOF	Totally destroyed, but undoubtedly wood beams spanned the nave with cane or saguaro ribs placed over these and covered with grass and finished with an adobe-mud roof.
EXTERIOR	Finish—plaster over burned brick and adobe.
INTERIOR	1/2″ mud plaster on adobe, whitewashed. In sanctuary—tile pattern marked off in plaster with painted decorations of Indian red.
STAIRS	Exterior, brick stairs to roof adjoining west wall at front of church.
BELFRY	Original wall belfry (espadaña) of brick over entrance—now destroyed.
OUTLYING BUILDINGS	Ruined living quarters of adobe stand in a line adjoining rear east wall of church.

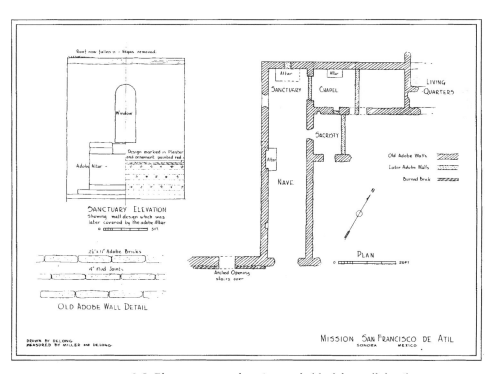

FIGURE 8.1. Plan, sanctuary elevation, and old adobe-wall detail.

CHAPTER NINE

Santa Teresa

Within a few miles northeast of Atil, on the west side of the road stand the ruins of Santa Teresa (Fig. 9.1). This was originally a visita of Tubutama. We visited this site twice; once on Sunday, 20 October, and again on 24 October.

The church proper, which faces southwest, was larger than that of Atil, and in the course of years the establishment extended in a rambling fashion north and east and southeast. Northeast of the chapel were a series of rooms which were evidently part of the cloister, or priest's quarters. Southeast, in a long row, were the simpler, more flimsy habitations of the neophytes. When the Franciscans took over the Jesuit property in 1768 the church at Santa Teresa was noted as being small and devoid of ornaments and having a house for the father. The Indian population at that time was fifty-two souls.[1]

In 1751–52 occurred the Pima uprising. Santa Teresa was headquarters of Sebastian, one of the Indian leaders who, with about one thousand rebel tribesmen fired the church and house. Consequently, this picturesque station, now isolated and partially hidden by brush and cactus, was at one time the scene of thrilling activity. Evidence of Apache raids is still to be seen in the presence of small arrowheads found in the ruins.

The chapel was built in the form of an L. The adobe bricks of which it was constructed were relatively thin, while the mud mortar with which they were cemented was thicker than the bricks themselves.

The sketch (Fig. 9.2) indicates the general plan of the mission. Owing to the almost complete disintegration of the neophytes' quarters, it was not possible to obtain accurate floor plans of those houses. Even the thicker

FIGURE 9.1. Ruins of the old mission church.

walls of the convento were difficult to trace with any degree of accuracy. The usual amount of broken pottery, stone implements, and fragmentary remains of European cultural material were scattered in profusion about this place. Here we made a type collection of artifacts, as we did at those sites where we could feel fairly certain that the later, mid-nineteenth-century specimens did not appear. No collection was made at Atil for the simple reason that there was too much surface debris of the nineteenth and twentieth centuries in evidence.

In the brush across the road from the mission, in the direction of the Altar River, which is but a few rods eastward from the old church, are many Indian hut sites which are apparently more ancient than those adjacent to the chapel proper. The whole area here gives mute evidence of having supported a large population.

In fact, the entire Altar Valley seems to have been well occupied by the Indians. In the low range of hills opposite the town of Oquitoa we saw the terraces of trincheras.[2] Broken pottery and artifacts may be picked up along this valley at many places. The region is well worth an intensive archaeological survey. While the Papago pottery seems to predominate, there are many shards of the ware commonly associated with the trincheras.

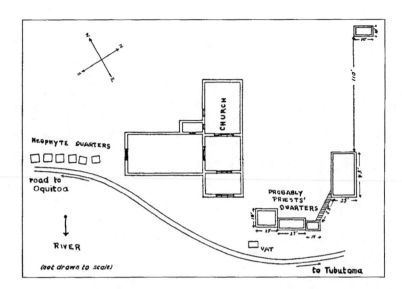

FIGURE 9.2. Mission site plan
(Woodward).

Similarly, the stone artifacts indicate a mixture of cultures. The small Apache arrowheads mingle with larger stone blades and Papago arrow straighteners. The pot shards show different degrees of weathering, and in many cases the camp sites are only discernible by the scattered fragments of pottery, broken fire stones, flakes, etc. The houses in such instances have long since disappeared.

We heard a rumor of a mill that had at one time belonged to Santa Teresa which was on the river southeast of the church. We visited this place but found it to be a mill erected sometime during the 1850s or 1860s, now in ruins, and the buildings occupied by a poor Mexican family. However, at this point are many old fruit and palm trees; the latter grow very tall, and are visible above the dense foliage of the river bottom. The Altar River, which is an intermittent stream, is dry along this particular stretch. There may be other fragmentary ruins of buildings once a part of the mission establishment along the river, but we did not have time to search for them.

It must be remembered that in all cases where these missions were established, *there must have been outlying buildings* [emphasis added] of one kind or another, depending upon the resources of that particular mission. Such industries as milling, tanning, brickmaking, lime burning, etc., were carried on. We found a small plastered vat almost directly in front of the living quarters of the priest at Santa Teresa, which may have been simply a small water reservoir. It was 7′ 2″ x 5′ 7″, the depth uncertain as we did not have time to excavate it.

ORIENTATION — West-northwest.[3]

CONDITION OF CHURCH — Portions of ruined walls standing from 4′ to 12′ high.

WALLS — Adobe brick with wide, adobe-mud joints.

ROOF — Destroyed but probably of the usual construction using wood ceiling beams, small poles, grass, and mud.

INTERIOR — Finish—thin mud plaster on adobe. No evidence of painted decorations located other than whitewash.

OUTLYING BUILDINGS — A series of rooms to the north and east of the church, in ruined condition with several small portions of adobe walls still standing above the debris. Other building foundations traceable north of church.

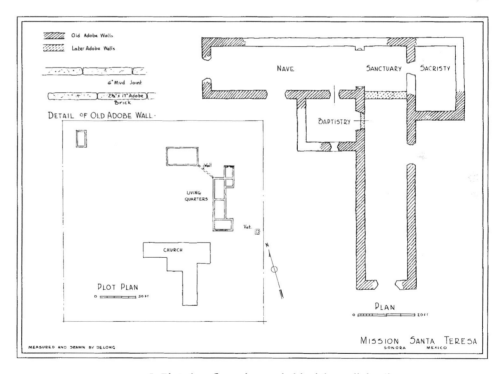

FIGURE 9.1. Plot plan, floor plan, and old adobe-wall detail.

FIGURE 10.1. Exterior from the northwest.

CHAPTER TEN

Nuestra Señora de la Concepción de Caborca

We determined to inspect this church before attempting Pitiquito or Tubutama, reserving those places for the last. Accordingly we obtained a letter of introduction from Sr. Escobar to Sr. Rafael Celaya, presidente of the *ayuntamiento* at Caborca, on 21 October and went directly to that town.

The present town of Caborca is modern in aspect as far as any of the towns may be said to be modern. Here are concentrated all of the activities of the area. The older pueblo which once clustered around the mission church is now a short distance to the east and is slowly decaying on the banks of the Asunción River [today known as the Río Concepción] which will ultimately engulf the crumbling adobes as it has gnawed away the rear portion of the splendid edifice erected by the Franciscans.

This mission was originally founded by Fr. Francisco Javier Saeta in October 1694.[1] He was slain by rebellious Indians of Tubutama, Oquitoa, and Santa Teresa early in the morning of 2 April 1695. Caborca seemed fated to play a bloody role in the history of the Western Altar district. On 20 November 1751, when the Pima rebels again swept down the valley with fire and arrows, Padre Tomás Tello fell a victim to their fury.

Still later, in 1857, the church was the scene of violent fighting when the townspeople of Caborca were driven into the old mission by a band of American filibusters headed by Henry A. Crabb. The action ended when Crabb and his men were smoked out of their adobe house-fort opposite the church, and surrendered to the Mexicans. The prisoners were promptly executed.[2]

Floods have long menaced the area. In 1771 the padres moved back from the river to a point on the wide plain, hoping to build in safety. The lands were excellent for cultivation of many types of crops. Cotton was raised here as early as 1740. The Indians wove cotton garments (*Documentos* 1853–1857, 841–42, [letter] by Jacobo Sedelmayr, written at Tubutama, 20 March 1747).[3]

In 1772 cotton was still an important crop but other items raised here were wheat, corn, barley, etc. There were extensive gardens in which grew quinces, pomegranates, peaches, lemons, oranges, and grapes. At that time the church was well decorated. The sacristy had two silver chalices, silver *vinagreras*, and a silver shell for baptism. The Indian population numbered 634.[4]

In 1772 Caborca had two visitas, San Antonio Pitiqui and San Juan del Bísanig.

The present structure (Fig. 10.1) is Franciscan in origin [1803–9]. Today, the church is a very sorry wreck (Fig. 10.2). Fully half of the fine structure, which is solidly built of stone and burned brick, and well plastered, inside and out, having a handsome facade, and two sturdy bell towers, has been destroyed by the river. The stream, which at certain times of the year foams down the sandy bed, has eaten away at the main altar and all of the structures that once stood in the rear of the building.[5] The remainder of the nave, which is in good condition, has been walled up at the east end and now serves for a school (Fig. 10.3). When we were there, a young schoolmaster had some forty-eight children under his care. The equipment was meager, and the doctrines being taught were strictly in accord with the communistic leanings of the Agrarian party now in control of the nation. One Mexican bystander confidentially told me in a bitter whisper, "They teach the children *no hay dios*" (there is no God). The textbook is patterned somewhat upon the Russian theories.[6]

The church at Caborca must have been an elaborately decorated structure prior to the flood. We obtained copies of photographs made by a Mexican photographer, 2 February 1895, on the occasion of the patron saint's day, and those pictures show the building prior to the destruction by the water (Fig. 10.4). The interior was evidently lavishly decorated with painted designs, but these, with a few exceptions, have been whitewashed. This reornamentation was probably done sometime late in the early nineteenth century. Likewise a certain amount of reconstruction must have been carried on at the same time. This we could see from alterations made on the side altars—and in the niches on either side of the large, cruciform

FIGURE 10.2. Flood damage, southeast
view from the river bed.

niche above the north, side altar. In the latter cases the niches had been
walled solidly and whitewashed. Most of the elaborate color work had
been concealed under a layer of whitewash.

Even in the main portion of the church this effacement of designs has
been carried out. There are a few exceptions: In the center of the first
dome of the nave is a modeled fish motif which is painted a copper green.
It would appear that the older painted designs were done in brick red,
copper green and blue, steel gray blue, and salmon pink, while the later
painting was done in vivid cobalt blue. Here and there the various colors

FIGURE 10.3. Nave, looking west toward entrance and choir loft, presently (1935) used as school.

peep through the whitewash, and by careful scaling we were able to obtain our firsthand knowledge of this change in decoration.

The church originally was cruciform in shape (see plan, Fig. 10.I) and was one of the most elaborate of the circuit; the only others comparable to it were San Xavier del Bac and Tubutama. In appearance, Caborca more closely resembles San Xavier,[7] except that the facade is not as ornate. Tubutama, while more elaborate inside, at present has lost a great deal of the gingerbread work[8] that once adorned the exterior front.

FIGURE 10.4. Facade as it was in 1895 during a holiday (Anon.).

FIGURE 10.5. Arcade on the north side of the church.

The church at Caborca faces almost due west, fronting on the dying remnants of the old pueblo where a few hardy souls yet live in defiance of their more progressive brothers who have moved further to the west and northwest.

On the north side of the church is part of an arcaded corridor (Fig. 10.5) which at one time was the portico of a row of rooms which probably gave on an inner garden. In line with the front of the church and extending north, along what is now the bank of Río Concepción, but which in ancient times must have been a fertile plain, were long rows of adobe structures. These may have been the houses of the neophytes or possibly workshops. The sites of these structures are now marked by low, badly eroded mounds, and stone foundations, visible where the encroaching river has eaten away the earth (Fig. 10.6).

Under the arches of the convento, as it was known, along the south wall of the corridor was a bench about 18″ high, well plastered and tinted red (see plan, Fig. 10.I). To the left of one of the doorways a similar bench about 23″ high formerly stood, but this has been destroyed. These features are mentioned because they tally with the benches which were along the inner corridor of the patio at Tumacacori on the east side of that mission church. Similar plastered benches were uncovered during the course of excavation in 1934–1935, and have since been covered with earth.[9]

It was in this convento on the north side of Caborca that the women and children of the town took refuge from the American *filibusteros* in the first part of April 1857. The Mexican version of the expedition attributes the failure of Crabb's attempt to blow up the convento to the miraculous appearance of the patron saint of the church.

We made as many observations on all parts of the building as our limited time permitted. From the bell tower we obtained a fine view of the surrounding terrain (Fig. 10.7). These towers are interesting, and the narrow stairways leading to them, even more so. The old tiles on the steps are so badly worn that one must be extremely careful; one is likely to stumble and fall. The sides of the passages are polished by the contact with countless numbers of persons who have climbed to the towers. Here again one senses a similarity in the approach to the towers at San Xavier del Bac, although these stairs are longer and have more arched passages.

In the lower part of the north tower are four bells. Two of these are lying on the floor of the tower; two are hanging cracked, and almost useless. Two were cast in 1898, one in 1816, and the fourth has no date on it. The oldest bell bears this inscription on the rim: "*Puryssyma Concepcyon de Maria An. de 1816.*" Evidently these bells were rung from below, outside

FIGURE 10.6. Rear of the church from the northeast.

the tower. This is graphically shown by the deep, narrow slots abraded in the burned brick of the outer edge of the facing of the bell-tower arches; here the ropes have slowly cut their way during the course of the years.

Scrawled on the inner walls of the towers are many names. In the south tower the oldest is "Juan Ricketson, 1854." Another "party" consists of, "D. W. Harvey, C. Y. Wimple, J. P. Gabriel, and J. Speedy, 1866." There were many visitors here during the 1870s, 1880s, and late 1890s. On 2 February 1892 a holy feast was held at Caborca, and among those who attended were [our friends] Alberto and F. Escobar. These men were also there 2 December 1888. Alberto Escobar was the artist (now living in Altar) who drew the ground plan and side elevation of the old church at Altar, since destroyed (see above, Figs. 6.1 & 6.2).

FIGURE 10.7. Bell tower and view from the roof.

The facade of this mission church is pitted in places with bullet marks. These are the mute reminders of the Crabb filibuster siege of April 1857, mentioned above. The plaster around the windows in the northern bell tower is badly chipped, and under one window (inside the tower) a loophole, gouged out by one of the defenders of the mission, is still visible.

There was no original furniture in the church. All of this has long since disappeared.

ORIENTATION	West.
CONDITION OF CHURCH	Rear portion including the sanctuary, sacristy, and south transept destroyed by floods, north transept left exposed (see above, Figs. 10.2 and 10.6). Nave—walled off and now used as a school (see above, Fig. 10.3).
FOUNDATIONS	Well-cemented rubble stone.
FLOORS	6″ x 13″ burned brick.
WALLS	Well-cemented stone and burned brick with brick facing.
CEILINGS	Nave and transepts—low brick domes between transverse brick arches. Crossing has a semicircular dome on high octagonal drum. Ceilings—plaster with plaster ornaments in centers of domes, shell-ornamented ceiling over choir loft.
EXTERIOR	Plaster over brick. Plaster ornament on entrance facade.
INTERIOR	Finish—whitewashed plaster. Whitewash covers early painted decorations on walls and ceiling.
DOORS	Molded-panel mesquite doors hung on wrought-iron hinges.
OUTLYING BUILDINGS	Mostly destroyed by river but a few foundations are still traceable. A plastered brick arcade remains adjoining the rear north wall of church; the front wall of a row of rooms back of the arcade still stands. Series of groined brick vaults form the ceiling of the arcade.

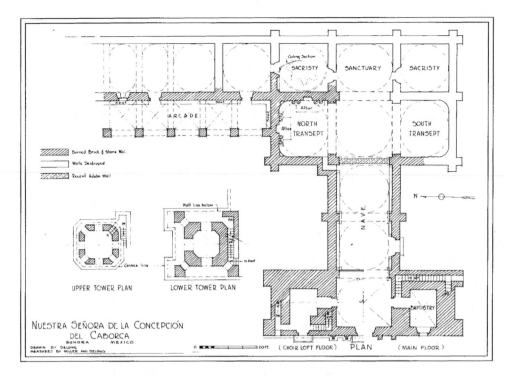

FIGURE 10.I. Plan, upper-tower plan, lower-tower plan.

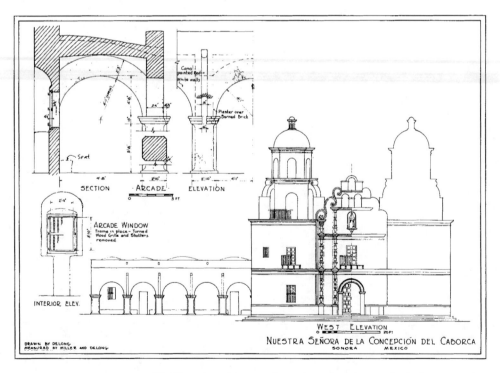

FIGURE 10.II. West elevation, arcade section, elevation, and window.

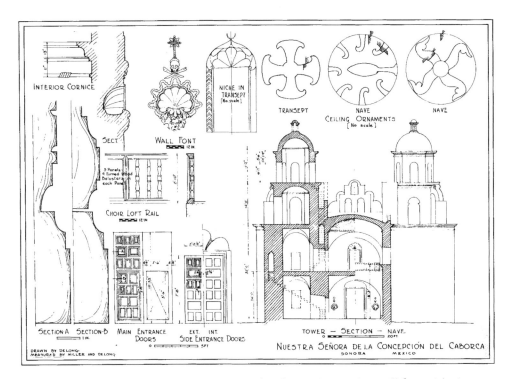

FIGURE 10.III. Cross section, details: interior cornice, wall font, niche in transept, ceiling ornaments, and entrance doors.

FIGURE 11.1. Exterior from the southwest.

CHAPTER ELEVEN

San Diego del Pitiquito

On Tuesday, 22 October 1935, we left Altar to make observations at this Mission. Pitiquito was founded by Kino sometime prior to October 1694. However, it was never of much importance, structurally speaking, until after the Franciscan accession of the Jesuit field. This mission was formerly a *ranchería* of Pitiqui attached to Caborca, and in the first half of the eighteenth century was known as la Natividad del Señor del Pitiqui (*Documentos* 1853–1857, 617–37). At that time, some ninety-six families lived there as well as sixty-seven widows and fifty-four orphans. In 1768, when the Franciscans took over the churches, the place was known as San Antonio Pitiqui, and there was neither church nor house for the priest at that place. Fr. Juan Díaz was the first Franciscan at this post, 1768–73. The present brick structure was built sometime between 1768 and 1778 (Fig. 11.1).

We arrived at the town and presented a note of introduction from Mr. Roy Cutting to his friend Manuel Tiznada, presidente of the pueblo. Sr. Tiznada was a butcher but an agreeable man withal. He assigned Francisco Bonillas, the comandante de policía, to our party. Sr. Bonillas took the key, opened the church, and stayed with us, giving such information as he had concerning the church and the town.

The templo stands on a small elevation facing west (Fig. 11.2). The modern town sprawls at the base of the hills in the rear of the church, and the scattered houses of the older pueblo lie in front of the structure. According to Bonillas, local tradition claims that the town takes its name from a famous Indian chieftain who once lived in the ranchería where the church was built. This leader, known as Piti or Pitic, fought against the

FIGURE 11.2. Main facade.

Spaniards but was ultimately whipped in a battle on a small fortified peak west of the church known as Sierra Quisuan. On this hill are the remnants of stone walls.

Another Indian chief identified with the history of the region was known as Cañedo, and a peak immediately west of the town bears his name. North of the church, rimming the horizon, are the low hills comprising the Sierra de Pitiquito. Here, in the western end, where the hills begin to diminish somewhat, a fight occurred on 11 April 1911 between the forces of Francisco Reyna, Madero adherents, and a rebel band. The *maderistas* won, and three or four soldiers were buried in the modern cemetery northwest of the town.

It is a solidly built edifice of stone and burned brick and in some respects differs from the other churches we visited. For example, the interior workmanship is solid, massive construction, especially the pulpit and the lectern. Both are built of pillars and arches (Fig. 11.3) which give an air of austere frigidity to the place that we did not encounter elsewhere.[1]

Although this church was constructed in the eighteenth century, there have been some "improvements" made at various times: In 1897, a new wooden floor was laid, the broad stone-and-concrete steps and platform

FIGURE 11.3. Interior—east wall of nave with side altar.

FIGURE 11.4. Window in the sacristy showing carved, triple-scallop head and masonry steps.

leading to the front entrance were constructed, and a new brick bell gable (espadaña) was added to the roof, with two bells, cast by T. Romero (probably of the same Romero family who lived in Tubutama, where the bells were more than likely cast).

At this same period, the main altar was reconstructed, a plain wooden affair being built over the brick-and-plaster original. Stained glass windows were also installed, and later, electric lights were added. The original main doors have long since disappeared, and much of the other woodwork is comparatively modern.

Of original furnishings, there are but a few remnants. In the small dark room at the base of the bell-tower stairs, on the north side of the building, we found a small, eighteenth-century *arca*, or wooden chest (Fig. 11.III). This was smaller than the one in the baptistry of San Ignacio (Fig. 3.7, above) but of the same type. The iron hasp and ornamental iron lock escutcheon were gone. At one time this chest had been covered with black leather, but even this had rotted away and had been pulled off, leaving only a few hard, dry scraps nailed along the sides of the body and lid. The chest was 34-1/2″ long, 15-1/2″ wide, and 14″ high.

In the sacristy was a large, old, eighteenth-century cupboard, or chest, with two paneled doors. This stood 43-1/2″ high, and was 30-1/2″ wide, and 58″ long (Fig. 11.III). These two objects were the only items visible pertaining to the days of the founding of this church. There were rumors of other pieces of furniture and fittings, which had been taken from the

FIGURE 11.5. Domed and vaulted arcade, link to *convento*.

FIGURE 11.6. Exterior from the rear showing remnants of adjoining buildings, now gone.

mission and were said to be in the possession of a pious lady of the town, but I could not obtain her name.

[The interior view of the high window in the sacristy (Fig. 11.4) may supplement a drawing, but it is far more interesting, because it shows the dramatic and functional light effect on the triple-scallop carved head above, and also the well-worn steps and seat built into the masonry recess.][2]

On the south side of the church was the convento. Here is the same domed, arched portico, or arcade (Fig. 11.5) as that found at Caborca, and that which probably stood on the inner side of the eastern patio at Tumacacori.[3] Some of the old rooms are here, in ruinous condition, but the main portions of the convento are gone, and only the heavy stone foundations are visible (see Fig. 11.I).

On one of the side doors of Pitiquito are two paper seals typical of those pasted on the doors of other churches closed by order of the Federal government. The seals, ordinary strips of bond paper, bear these words typewritten on them, "Pitiquito, Dcre. 15 de 1934 sellado per orden Superior."

Our preliminary survey of Pitiquito was soon finished, and we decided to push on to our next objective.

San Diego del Pitiquito: Outline Description

ORIENTATION	West.
CONDITION OF CHURCH	Fairly well preserved.
FOUNDATIONS	Rubble stone in cement.
FLOORS	Brick, now covered by newer wood floor.
WALLS	Burned brick and stone with brick facing and molded brick cornice.
CEILINGS	Barrel-vaulted ceiling in nave and baptistry. Half dome over sanctuary. Pear-shaped dome on pendentives over the crossing.
EXTERIOR	Finish—whitewashed plaster on brick. Painted decorations around entrance.
ARCADE	Burned-brick piers and arches with vaulted ceilings between transverse arches.
INTERIOR	Finish—whitewashed plaster. Earlier painted decorations now covered over with whitewash.
DOORS	Paneled mesquite doors hung on iron pins.
OUTLYING BUILDINGS	Foundations of rooms and continuation of the arcade traceable adjoining south wall at front of church. Evidence of other rooms adjoining rear of church.

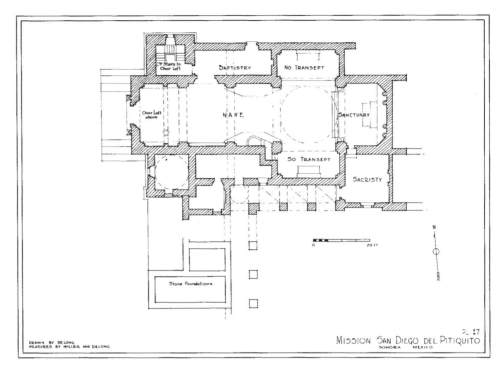

FIGURE 11.I. Plan.

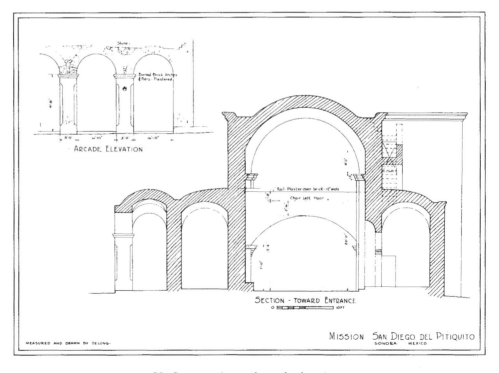

FIGURE 11.II. Cross section and arcade elevation.

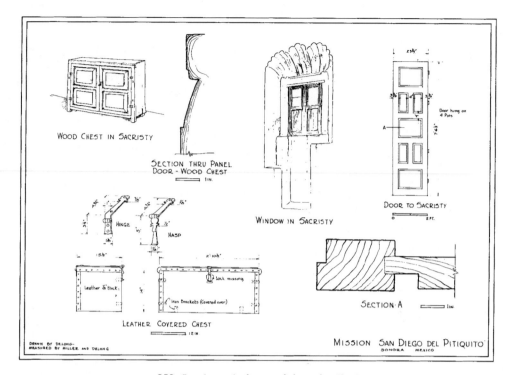

FIGURE 11.III. Sacristy window and door details.

CHAPTER TWELVE

San Juan del Bísanig
(San Valentín)

This was a visita of Caborca and is sometimes known as San Valentín or plain Bísani [without a *g*]. Another name was Nuestra Señora del Pópulo.[1] The mission apparently was flourishing in 1768. In 1772, it was described [by Reyes] as being six leagues west of Caborca and having a church and a house for the priest, but the former was unadorned and the latter unfurnished.

This visita was the headquarters of some of the Pima rebels who fled here after 1751. In the beginning of 1772, after more trouble, some of the population fled to the hills. It seems always to have been a center for troublesome spirits and, being on the fringe of the mission settlements, it offered a haven to renegades. By nature, the spirit of the outpost of Bísanig was restless. Although the farm lands were excellent, the Indians dwelling there preferred to live by fishing in the sea, which was some eight or ten leagues distance from the ranchería.[2] Today, this preference is borne out by the quantity of shells scattered over the occupational area of Bísanig. In fact, of all the sites visited, this one indicates most plainly the affiliation of the inhabitants with maritime industry. No other mission has so many shells around it.

The mission church, although a simple adobe structure, built with two wings, one being the baptistry, the other the sacristy, having a small patio on the west side between these two, was not without a certain charm in arrangement which must have made life a trifle more easy in that desolate outland of deserted plain and sterile hills.

As may be seen in the accompanying sketch of the ground plan (Fig. 12.1), the chapel faces south. The mission stands on a level, alluvial plain.

The lands are known as being of the *tierra temporal*, watered only by intermittent rains. The present well, which furnishes water to the ranch house occupied by Sr. Macedonio Yáñez, caretaker of the ranch owned by Sr. Pedro Gonzáles, is 200′ deep, giving some idea of the water level at this place. In Caborca, the water is close to the surface.

The passing years and the indefatigable spades of the treasure hunters have dealt harshly with San Valentín. The walls now standing are badly eroded but are high enough to indicate the approximate size of the building, as it appeared when in good condition (Fig. 12.2). Although the edifice was built of adobe bricks, a certain amount of burned tile and burned bricks—fired in a kiln which stood 150 yards or more to the southwest of the chapel—was used. The main altar, now totally demolished by gold hunters was of burned brick, and chances are the flooring was of fired tile.

The nave of the chapel was about 73′ long and 15′10″ wide. The wing in which the baptistry was housed was 26′ long, and perhaps 12′ or 14′ in width. The sacristy was smaller. Along the north side of the baptistry wall extended a portico, the roof of which was composed of brush, grass, and adobe held up by adobe pillars. This sun shade was 12′ to 14′ wide. In the

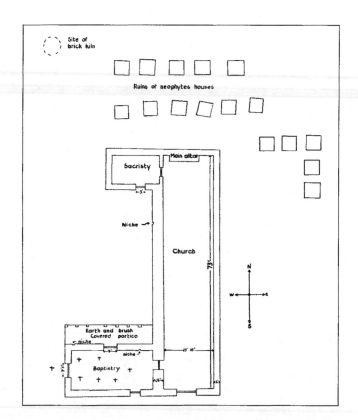

FIGURE 12.1. Mission site plan, no scale (Woodward).

FIGURE 12.2. Ruins of adobe walls.

wall of the baptistry, sheltered by the roof of the colonnade, were a series of small plastered niches. One of these could be identified. In this niche was the fragment of a molded, plastered crucifix. Apparently these niches extended along the wall of the baptistry and the west wall of the main church, as we found traces of one of the niches on the latter wall. Judging by the remnants of plaster, one could see that the building had undergone renovation several times. The primary coats were the usual poor, thin, whitewash plaster, but the last finish was fairly hard. This was best in evidence at the circular window in the south wall of the baptistry. Here the plaster had clung to the adobe casing of the window and was still in excellent condition.

At Bísanig, as well as at all the other sites, the treasure hunters had been at work. Gaping holes in the floor, total destruction of the main altar, and undermined walls gave a graphic picture of their foolish industry.

West and northwest of the chapel were the long rows of adobe and wattle-and-daub huts occupied by the neophytes. These have long since disintegrated leaving only the lines of stone foundations, the masses of broken pottery, fragments of stone implements, and many sea shells such as glycimeris, turatella, and conus. The pottery fragments here are typically Papago, and I did not see the Trincheras ware, at least not in the quantities so prevalent on sites in the vicinity of Altar, San Ignacio, Cocóspera, Dolores, Imuris, etc.

Owing to the out-of-the-way location of this mission, few tourists visit the place; consequently, the camp debris is practically as it was when the last Indians moved away. I believe from certain evidences of material culture found on the ground that the Papago lived here until about the middle of the nineteenth century, long after the missions had been abandoned. Even now the crude wooden crosses made by the Christianized Indians stand thickly planted over the poor native burials inside the slowly dying walls of the baptistry.

It took many years to plant the seeds of Christianity in that harsh land, and now the vines thus planted are slow to perish. Even though the ministering influence has become but a memory, the Indians cling tenaciously to the precepts taught their forefathers by those hardy toilers in the vineyard of God.[3]

The road to Bísanig is rather difficult to follow. Leaving Caborca, one turns to the southeast and follows the main traveled highway, if such it may be called, which gradually bears away southwest across a series of low flats, thence through a low range of hills and out into more brush-covered flats. The trail winds through heavy brush and emerges on a grassy flat. This is about 10 miles from town. Here is a junction of the roads. The traveler seeking the mission takes the left-hand branch and follows it to Rancho Bísanig where Sr. Yáñez holds forth. This ranch is about 15 miles southwest of Caborca. Only one gate has to be opened along this road.[4]

About 9 miles west of Caborca, on the south side of the road, a point of rocks juts out from a low, rocky ridge. Here are many fine Indian petroglyphs which will repay anyone interested in such matters.

San Juan del Bísanig (San Valentín): Outline Description

ORIENTATION   South.

CONDITION OF CHURCH   Portions of ruined walls standing from 2′ to 12′ high.

WALLS   Adobe brick with wide adobe-mud joints.

ROOF   Totally destroyed but undoubtedly constructed in the typical manner using wood beams, small poles, grass, and mud.

INTERIOR   Thin, mud plaster over adobe, whitewashed. Traces of painted decoration near altar location in sanctuary.

EXTERIOR   Evidence of a ramada with adobe piers and brush roof along north wall of baptistry. Several niches remain in the exterior walls that form a patio in front of the ramada.

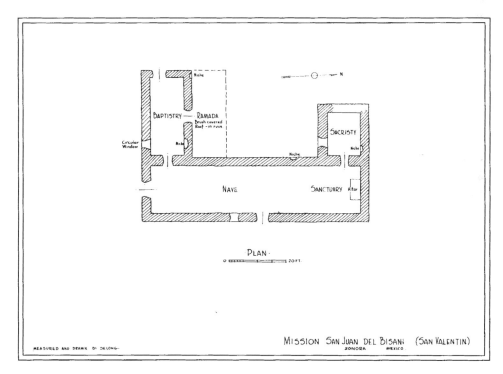

FIGURE 12.1. Plan.

FIGURE 13.1. Exterior from the southeast.

CHAPTER THIRTEEN

San Pedro y San Pablo de Tubutama

This mission lies north of Oquitoa in the same Altar Valley, about 21 miles from the latter town. The church stands on top of a hill from which a pleasant view is had in all directions. To the northwest is the Sierra San Juan, to the southwest Santa Teresa. The river flows along the base of the hill to the south. The town of Tubutama clusters around the church and the plaza upon which the edifice fronts (Fig. 13.1). In the valley are the broad fertile fields producing luxuriously all manner of crops, as indeed all the flat lands of the Río Altar seem to do. Here in times past, the padres must have had great success with their agricultural endeavors between Apache raids and rebellious Pima and Papago neophytes.[1]

We journeyed to Tubutama on 24 October. We found the presidente a bit suspicious, nothing overt, just an air of aloofness not displayed by other officials with whom we had come in contact. However, after we chatted with him for awhile, he became more agreeable and stayed with us (as some of the other officials usually did——in hopes of tips, and to see that we did not steal the churches stone by stone).

The nave of the church faces east. However, the main entrance into the narthex fronts on the south (see the plan, Fig. 13.I). The building as it stands is probably of Franciscan origin (1788),[2] with walls of adobe faced with burned brick. But the mission was founded by the Jesuits under Kino (ca. 1689–91).[3] For many years it was an important link in the Kino circuit and had for its visitas, Santa Teresa, Atil, Oquitoa, and probably the presidial church in Altar.

In 1730, according to the author of "Estado de la Provincia de Sonora" (*Documentos* 1853–1857, 617–37), which gives a descriptive list of all the towns, churches, and missionaries in Sonora in 1730, Tubutama had four towns under its jurisdiction. At the mission itself there were forty-two families, twenty-two widows, and twenty-five orphans. In 1768 Tubutama was flourishing, the church was well supplied with all the necessary paraphernalia for conducting church services, and the house of the fathers was neat and spacious with a good garden. There were 176 people at the mission, and the natives were actively employed raising wheat, corn, and beans, although as agriculturists they seem not to have had too much ambition.

Here on 29 March 1695 began the Pima uprising when the Indians of the Altar Valley attacked a group of Opatas brought in to aid in the work at Tubutama. They slew three of these alien tribesmen at Tubutama, and then the rebels moved south to attack Caborca. As it so happened, Padre Daniel Januske, in charge of Tubutama, was away from the place when the murders occurred, which probably saved his life. As it was, Padre Francisco Javier Saeta, resident priest at Caborca, fell a victim to the fury of the warriors.

The mission at Tubutama suffered at this time. The Indians set fire to the house and chapel, and destroyed images, pictures, and vestments.[4] However, in the years that followed, Tubutama regained strength and was prominent in the church history of the Altar district for many years. The famous Spanish explorer, Juan Bautista de Anza (1735–88), who founded San Francisco, visited Tubutama in January 1774 en route to California.[5]

In the year 1781, on 17 July and 19 July, four Franciscan missionaries— Fr. Francisco Garcés, age 43; Fr. Juan Antonio Barreneche, his assistant, 32 years old; Fr. Juan Díaz, 45 years of age; and Fr. José Matías Moreno, 37 years—all stationed at the Yuma mission on the banks of the Colorado, near the mouth of the Gila River, were slain by the Yumas. An expedition was sent to find the bodies and transport them to Tubutama. The bones of the four priests were placed in one box and carried to the mission where, "after the usual ceremonies, they received a most honorable burial on the Epistle side of the main altar" (Englehardt 1899, 147–48). Bolton (1930, 2: 72) states that the bodies of Garcés and Díaz lie in Tubutama, but Englehardt (1899, 151) asserts, "Some years later the relics were taken to the mother-house at Querétaro and there solemnly interred on 19 July 1794. A sermon on the virtues and merits of his four martyrs was delivered in Spanish by Father Diego Miguel Bringas de Manzaneda y Encinas, OFM, and another in Latin by Father José María Carranza." Thus, it would seem that the mortal remains of the famous California padre Francisco Garcés lie in Querétaro rather than Tubutama.[6]

An examination of the present church at Tubutama indicates many changes in construction. The interior is more elaborate than any of the other churches in the circuit. It has a main altar and two side altars. The two side altars are of heavy mesquite wood which has been plastered over. They are covered with a multitude of molded designs (Figs. 13.2 and 13.3).

FIGURE 13.2. South transept, side altar.

FIGURE 13.3. North transept, side altar.

The one on the left of the main altar [i.e., the south transept] is decorated with all the symbols of the crucifixion. Here may be seen, in bas-relief, representations of the spear and sponge, hammer, pincers, cross of thorns, the flail, and the ladder.

The main altar was apparently of painted and gilded woodwork, but all portions of this elaborate structure have been stripped away. The nave cornice [classical] is covered with painted ornaments (Figs. 13.4 and 13.III). The colors are fairly brilliant, and the patterns stand out in greenish black, and vermilion. The base of the dome over the crossing is also lavishly decorated (Figs. 13.5 and 13.II). However, as with many interiors, the total effect is more bizarre than one of good taste.[7]

As intimated in previous paragraphs, this edifice has seen many changes. The walls of the structure have evidently been heightened. This was done when the choir loft was installed. As one stands on the floor of the loft, the ends of the old supporting roof timbers are visible—flush with the wall on either side—where they were sawed off to give headroom to the choir. This loft has an interesting railing, details of which were sketched by DeLong (Fig. 13.I).

FIGURE 13.5. Looking up into decorated base (drum) of dome (WACC).

FIGURE 13.4. Sanctuary, south wall showing nave cornice.

Other evidences of reconstruction at Tubutama show up in the addition of the bell tower,[8] and the burned-brick facade which at one time was—and still is, to a certain extent—lavishly decorated with an embroidery of molded brick and plaster motifs, which in turn were painted (Figs. 13.6 and 13.7). In the sacristy is a window which gives evidence of having been remodeled at least three times. Originally the window (Fig. 13.8) was in the shape of sketch (A). Then, when the veneer was added to the outside, it was changed to conform to the shape indicated in (B), and now has been shortened inside to the form in (C) with modern glass panes and muntin bars.

A unique feature found in this church, but not observed elsewhere, was the presence of a number of carved and painted wooden replicas of pomegranates stuck in the plaster ceiling under the choir loft (Fig. 13.9). These peculiar ornaments cling to the ceiling like so many darts thrust there by some mischievous boy and are noticeable the moment one enters the main door of the church. This ceiling is badly cracked, has been for some time, and a sturdy mesquite timber with diagonal braces has been planted in the center of the nave floor to reinforce the elliptical ceiling vault supporting the choir-loft floor (Fig. 13.10). Local tradition has it that a priest lies buried here.

Four bells hang in the lower-story arches of the bell tower. One was cast in 1740, a second in 1742, a third in 1875 and a fourth, a smaller bell,

FIGURE 13.6. Facade, *facing page,* highly decorated.

FIGURE 13.7. Detail of Fig. 13.6 (Boundey).

had no date. The flooring of the upper portion of the tower has rotted away, and not having a strong ladder, I was unable to reach the four bells hanging in the upper arches to decipher the dates. In 1925 parts of the bell tower and roof were repaired, but the platforms were left untouched.

The steps leading through the narrow passageway onto the roof are badly worn and in places scarred with soot from candle flames. Here too, on the ledges of the bell-tower arches, one observes the deep slots cut by the bell cords, and by lining up the direction of the cuts with the bells and the ground, one is able to determine the spot whereon the bell ringers stood.

In the entrance to the choir loft, which one reaches by three short flights of tiled stairs, the flooring is composed of flat triangular adobe bricks. These triangular bricks were found *only* [emphasis added] at this place. Here, on the smooth plastered walls and ceiling of these narrow arched stairways, the streaks of candle smoke have left their grimy marks.

In many respects Tubutama has much more such personal touches of the former inhabitants than some of the other missions. Caborca, ruined and used as a school has but a slight trace of such feeling; heavy, solid Pitiquito—with the bat flight flittering endlessly from the dark maw of the pulpit entrance to the domed ceiling and back in the approved style of a haunted edifice—lacks the human touch; San Ignacio perhaps most nearly approaches it; and even ruined San Valentín has that indefinable something which bespeaks the presence of its former occupants. *But here in Tubutama, one senses the unseen aura shed by the builders* [emphasis added].

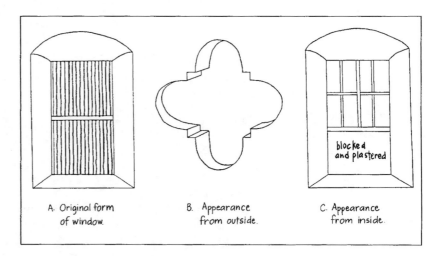

FIGURE 13.8. Detail of window in the sacristy (Woodward).

A. Original form of window.

B. Appearance from outside.

C. Appearance from inside.

blocked and plastered

FIGURE 13.9. Narthex, doorway to baptistry, opposite main entrance.

FIGURE 13.10. Nave, looking east toward narthex and choir loft.

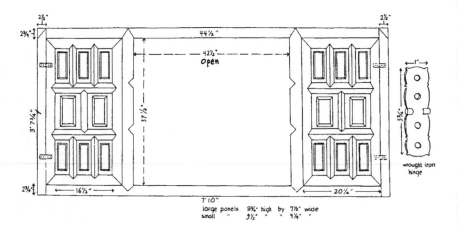

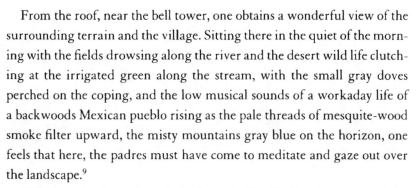

FIGURE 13.11. *Armario*, eighteenth-century combination table and cabinet (Woodward).

FIGURE 13.12. Ambry, or wall cupboard in the sacristy.

From the roof, near the bell tower, one obtains a wonderful view of the surrounding terrain and the village. Sitting there in the quiet of the morning with the fields drowsing along the river and the desert wild life clutching at the irrigated green along the stream, with the small gray doves perched on the coping, and the low musical sounds of a workaday life of a backwoods Mexican pueblo rising as the pale threads of mesquite-wood smoke filter upward, the misty mountains gray blue on the horizon, one feels that here, the padres must have come to meditate and gaze out over the landscape.[9]

Tubutama has been despoiled of practically all of its furniture and fittings, as have the majority of the churches. San Ignacio alone is rich in pictures, statues, vestments, and odds and ends of paraphernalia.

In the sacristy is a piece of furniture with two paneled doors known as an *armario* (Fig. 13.11). This is a good eighteenth-century item and indicates in what manner, and how solidly those old builders manufactured even the most homely bits of furniture for use in their frontier churches and homes. This heavy, combination cupboard and table is 7′10″ long, 42″ high, and 34-1/2″ deep. There were two compartments with a single shelf. The entire piece was constructed of mesquite, a wood which seems to last indefinitely. There were two original iron hinges on each door of the pattern shown in the sketch. These hinges were 3-3/4″ long and 1″ wide. The doors were paneled as indicated in the sketch.

Built in the north side of the sacristy wall was an ambry or cupboard (Fig. 13.12), which even in its partially ruined state showed the care lavished upon it. At one time it contained many little compartments, and according to Duell, the colors were quite vivid in 1921. It was suggestive in its arrangement of the early-eighteenth-century *vargueños*. George

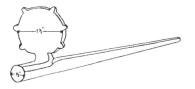

FIGURE 13.13. Wrought-iron picture
hanger (Woodward).

FIGURE 13.14. Plaster relief ornament on
the flat-dome nave ceiling (WACC).

Grant photographed both specimens of furniture. Even the iron picture
hangers which were driven into the walls were decorated (Fig. 13.13).

At one time there were many buildings surrounding this church, but
these have been destroyed. South of the chapel, in line with the church
building, was the convento and the quadrangle so often found in association with the larger mission establishments. Only the foundations of part
of this are now visible. A new school building has been erected on this site,
and the outline of some of the old foundation walls may be seen in the
front and rear of this modern structure.

ORIENTATION	Unique. An east-west nave, facade and entrance on south.
CONDITION OF CHURCH	Good.
FOUNDATIONS	Rubble stone in cement.
FLOORS	Burned brick 10″ and 11″ square. Triangular tiles in choir-loft floor.
WALLS	Burned brick, stone and adobe, showing different periods of construction and additions.
CEILINGS	Groined brick vaults between transverse brick arches in nave. Barrel vaults in transepts and sacristy. All ceilings highly decorated with plaster relief ornament (Fig. 13.14). Dome over crossing on high octagonal drum (see above, Fig. 13.5). Ceiling under choir loft studded with gilded carved wood pomegranates.
EXTERIOR	Plaster over brick with plaster relief decoration on the entrance facade.
INTERIOR	Plaster on brick, whitewashed up to nave cornice which is *lively* [emphasis added] with painted decoration. Dome, drum, cornice, and pendentives over the crossing show somewhat faded, but *interesting painted decoration* [emphasis added]. Choir-loft rail is of early date as indicated by crudely hand-carved balusters.
OUTLYING BUILDINGS	Foundations of former buildings to west of church now utilized by new school buildings, however some foundations and walls not so used are still traceable.

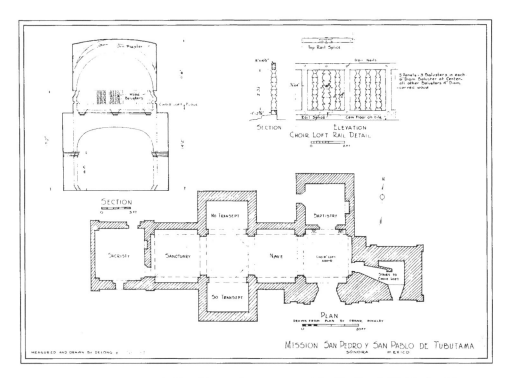

FIGURE 13.1. Plan (drawn from a 1920 original by Frank Pinkley), with a cross section, and choir-loft rail detail.

FIGURE 13.II. Detail of cornice below dome. (see Fig. 13.5)

FIGURE 13.III. Detail of nave cornice. (see Fig. 13.4)

CHAPTER FOURTEEN

Nuestra Señora de los Dolores

This was the mother mission of all the Pimería Alta, founded by Father Kino in March 1687. It is strategically situated (Fig. 14.1) on a high point of land with the opulent, level, lowland fields of the River San Miguel stretching away on both sides from the base of the rocky tongue upon which the mission establishment was built.[1]

As with many of the missions, Dolores "just grew." Building activities are indicated as early as April 1687, and by 1689 Dolores was reported as having a church, house, and rich fields planted to crops. On 26 April 1693 the new church at Dolores was dedicated. However, in the years that followed Kino's death, Dolores began to go downhill. By 1730 the missions of Sonora were in a dilapidated state. Later they rallied, and flourished again; but Dolores was abandoned in 1762 because of the unhealthy climate.

On Monday, 28 October, we left our temporary headquarters at the Cutting ranch for Dolores. En route to Magdalena, from Altar, we halted at La Playa to examine an archaeological site. This was particularly interesting for the reason that here, on a wide alluvial plain, within three hundred yards of the Santa Ana-Altar highway, is an ancient camp and workshop site whereon were manufactured hundreds of the shell bracelets traded so widely throughout the pueblo region of Arizona and New Mexico.

Apparently the Indians lived on this ground for centuries. A wide area is covered with broken stone implements, pottery shards, and hundreds of rough ovals cut from the centers of glycimeris shells, brought many weary miles on foot from the Gulf of California, probably from the vicinity of Bahía Kino or Puerto Libertad. Seasonal rains have cut arroyos through the silt deposit wherein these artifacts are buried, and as the soft earth washes away, the heavier objects tend to settle in irregular layers and masses. These deposit on the harder substrata where they may be gathered by the hundred. From this point the finished bracelets and earrings were carried hundreds of miles to the north and east and are now found in ancient pueblo sites in great numbers.[2]

About 2.5 miles southeast from this place is the long, low hill covered with rows of rocky terraces which were once the foundation of the *jacales* of the Indians inhabiting the hill. This is the famous "Las Trincheras" concerning which a great many references have been made, but no accurate analysis of the place has yet been written. As a matter of fact, there are many such trincheras in Sonora and extending into Arizona.[3]

Eleven miles from the Cutting ranch on the south side of the Santa Ana-Altar road is a small trinchera, about .5 mile distant from the highway. South of the town of Magdalena, 3.7 miles on the east side of the Magdalena-Santa Ana road is another fair-sized trinchera, and 10.8 miles south of the same town is yet another of these sites. Fifteen miles east of Magdalena on the rough and rocky road to Dolores Canyon is a steep conical peak which has many excellent rock terraces on it. The appearance of the masonry from the highway seems unusually firm and well built.[4]

These are but a few of the sites which we saw from the automobile. No attempt at examination was made. We had no time, and I cite these examples and locations to indicate the wealth of such material awaiting investigation. From such villages Kino and his associates, as well as the later Franciscan priests, drew their neophytes—in addition to the round, wattle-and-daub huts of the Pima and Papago.

We camped for the night in Dolores Canyon within a few miles of the ruins. This spot was known locally as "Santa Clara." Here on the west side of the stream, high on the old river terrace were the remains of a two-story rock house, the outline of a huge corral some 250' x 300', and closer to the river, the outlined foundations of four or five small houses, about 10' x 15' in size. The corral and house gave evidence of having been there for many years. Cut in the rocks northeast of the house we found a date, "1818." Lichens grew thickly on the rocks comprising the walls of the habitation.

The corral had been constructed in a rather peculiar manner. Stone pillars had been built about 10' apart and poles had evidently been laid between these pillars; the latter had either tumbled to the ground or been carried away by later settlers. Sr. José María Andrada and his family oc-

FIGURE 14.1. Site. Old building foundations still discernible.

cupy this place at the present time. Their ranch house stands near the river, and I was informed that this spot was healthier than other places further upstream. Sr. Andrada was the one who directed me to the ruins mentioned. The corral at present is screened in a tangle of mesquites.

Sonora is full of such abandoned places, and one is always wondering about them. Since Dolores was abandoned by the few remaining families in 1762, might this not have been the site selected by them? Or was this one of the cattle-ranch outposts of the mission proper? Why and whence the name Santa Clara? On this place I found several small fragments of blue and white majolica ware of the late eighteenth century, which seems to lend favor to the occupation in 1762 or thereabouts.

On the morning of 29 October we continued on to Dolores. We found the whole site a mass of tangled brush and scattered walls. Of the old church not a standing wall remains. In fact, we debated as to the actual

FIGURE 14.2. Site. Archaeologist (author Woodward) holds a carved stone block [possibly a capital].

site itself. There are two or three places where such buildings might have stood, if one is to judge by the width of the foundations discernible at several points (see above, Fig. 14.1).

From Kino's meager accounts of the building of Dolores we know that at least two churches stood here in his own time; how many more afterwards, it is difficult to decide. Personally, I believe the old church stood well out on the rocky point and faced southwest—looking down the valley. This is the traditional spot, and here in 1911 Dr. Bolton found standing walls. The church was of stone, but the rancheros of the region have hauled it away for building purposes. One piece of worked stone, which might well have been part of a carved capital for a small pillar (Fig. 14.2), surmounts a grave in the confines of the old quadrangle, further out on the point toward the southwest, where the terrain is more open, and freer from rocks. It may be that a later edifice stood near the quadrangle, which is traced only by the broad mounds of adobe, and stone foundations visible on the surface.

The truth of Dolores will never be known until the trowel and brush of the archaeologist is brought into play. The same is true of many of the other sites. Dolores in its prime was a huge, complex establishment. The church, living quarters, shops, storerooms, etc., covered several acres of ground, and there may be more ruins within the surrounding area which we did not have time to locate. Somewhere near at hand must be the remnants of the old mission gardens. Probably these are along the river.

One can easily understand why this site was chosen for a mission. It had all the requisites for a successful mission: a running stream; extensive, flat river bottomlands; timber along the lowlands; stone for building purposes; an elevated site capable of defense from invaders; and a large indigenous population.[5]

From our point of view, we learned very little at this site. No one could do justice to it, or make accurate deductions, without first excavating within the confines of the foundations and the mounded remains seen on every hand. George Grant, our photographer, took a number of views for future use in constructing dioramas for the proposed museum at the Tumacacori National Monument in Arizona. Also, the team posed for his camera.

FIGURE 14.3. Site. Members of the Sonora
Expedition on their final day in the field.
Left to right: Rose, Grant, Miller, Tovrea,
Woodward, and DeLong.

FIGURE 15.1. Exterior from the southeast.

FIGURE 15.2. View toward the old pueblo plaza from the church front.

CHAPTER FIFTEEN

Los Santos Reyes de Cucurpe

This was the last mission site visited by our party, aside from a brief inspection of the adobe mounds that once were Mission Imuris. There was a mission establishment at Cucurpe in 1650, thirty years before Kino established Dolores. In fact it was from Cucurpe that Kino plunged into the northern wilderness, and at that time Cucurpe was the northernmost outpost of the Spanish culture in Sonora.[1]

The country round about was rich with minerals, and settlers penetrated the region seeking the precious metals. In 1678 there was a village of one hundred and seventy families of Spanish and gente de razón, or better-class people aside from the Indians. However, by 1770 only five Indian families remained at this old place. The Indians in this part of the San Miguel Valley were not Piman, but of the Opata and Eudeve tribes, and seemingly allied with the natives of the Mission Opodepe in customs and language.

We left Dolores [on 29 October] and proceeded directly south to Cucurpe. The church, with its impressive series of brick arches, still stands in a half-finished condition on top of the hill overlooking the modern town of Cucurpe (Fig. 15.1). The old pueblo, built around the large plaza upon which the uncompleted stone church faces, has been practically abandoned for about fourteen years (Fig. 15.2). At that time a severe rainstorm caused most of the old adobe houses to crumble away, and now only half a dozen are habitable, and the road which once led up the slope from the southwest is so badly rutted that wheeled vehicles cannot traverse it.

At Cucurpe we found many evidences of reconstruction. The present church is built of volcanic tuff, burned brick, and adobe. Apparently, this structure was never finished but the arches effectively define the space (Fig. 15.3). Even in its incomplete state it is an imposing edifice, and if it is ever finished, as we heard townspeople rumor that someday it might be, it would make a fine-looking church. The residents of the pueblo have managed to keep parts of the adobe walls in repair, but in times past, other residents of the same village have helped themselves freely to the cut stone slabs which once were part of this chapel (Fig. 15.4).

There have been three church structures at Cucurpe. The first, and the oldest, was of adobe, and stood to the west and slightly to the rear of the present building. Only fragments of this mission church now remain, and these have been incorporated in the ruined houses of the natives. Here and there we saw stray items such as a crude baptismal font, bits of worked stone built into residential walls, and the ever-present stone foundations marking the site of the original church.

The second church still stands to the east of the unfinished stone church. This was a long, adobe building with the main entrance facing south, as did the entrances of all three churches (see plan, Fig. 15.I). This adobe building was apparently the one described by the writer [Antonio de los Reyes] in 1772. It was well decorated, had four altars, and was equipped with pictures and banners.

FIGURE 15.4. Architectural cut-stone fragments from the unfinished church.

It is well built of earth with a roof of good wood and grass, four chalices in the sacristy, a tall crucifix, four candlesticks and a lamp, all of silver, and plenty of other furnishings. The priest's house forms an interior patio with the church and is a huge and good house, made of adobe, and although it is new, some parts of it are going to ruin. The town of the Indians forms a plaza with the church and houses of the missionary; some are made of adobe but very low in appearance, not the regular height of a man, generally very poorly furnished and temporary in nature. In times past they have neglected their fields for *placeres*; there were 286 souls at the pueblo then.[2]

A site purporting to be the old Indian ranchería of Cucurpe was pointed out to me as existing on a hill some 1.5 miles south of the present town of Cucurpe, on the east side of the valley. The townspeople also assert that the old neophyte houses, attached to the mission, were in line with the second church and extended further to the east (plot plan, Fig. 15.1). There were some ruins in that direction, but I did not examine them. So many changes have taken place here that it would take time, patience, and some excavation to arrive at any reasonably accurate conclusion.

Of cultural objects pertaining to the church proper there were none, save a crudely carved baptismal font in the repaired sacristy room of the stone church which was in use apparently prior to the Federal order to close the churches. There were no chests, images, vestments, etc., only a few tawdry remnants of processional canopies, poles, crucifix, etc., all decidedly modern.

FIGURE 15.3. Interior, a view, *left,* from the sanctuary toward the entrance.

FIGURE 15.5. Brick arches, *right,* define the nave and the west transept.

Los Santos Reyes de Cucurpe: Outline Description

ORIENTATION	South for all three.
CONDITION OF CHURCHES	Three, built in different periods.
	First church—stone foundations remain.
	Second church—most adobe walls still stand.
	Third church—unfinished with walls partially completed and transverse, brick arch ribs in place.
FOUNDATIONS	Stone for all three.
WALLS	First church—adobe.
	Second church—adobe.
	Third church—faced with stone slabs to height of 4′ with adobe walls above.
ROOFS	First and second churches—probably typical wooden beams, poles, grass, and mud.
	Third church—transverse ribs of burned brick in nave.
	Sacristy roof supported on vigas.
INTERIORS	Second church—thin mud plaster, whitewashed.
	Third church—lime plaster.
STAIRS	Third church—circular stone stairs, impressive masonry (Fig. 15.6).
OUTLYING BUILDINGS	Line of adobe buildings on east and west sides of plaza, fronting the last two churches. These buildings are in varying stages of repair, desertion, and ruin.

FIGURE 15.6. Circular stairs in stone construction.

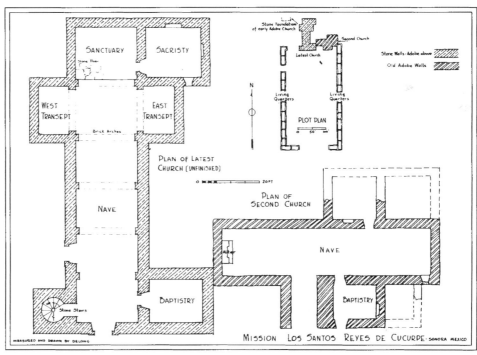

FIGURE 15.1. Plans of two churches and plot plan.

CHAPTER SIXTEEN

Los Santos Angeles de Guevavi
(in Arizona)

Outline Description

ORIENTATION	South.
CONDITION OF CHURCH	Ruined walls, parts of which are standing from 5′ to 12′ high.
FOUNDATIONS	Stone.
WALLS	Adobe bricks 4″ thick with 3″ mud joints.
ROOF	Destroyed but probably the typical early mission type constructed of wood beams spanning the nave and covered by small poles, grass, and mud.
INTERIOR	Thin mud plaster, whitewashed, light red color decoration remaining in a few places.
OUTLYING BUILDINGS	Stone foundations of a building to the east across a dry wash are traceable. Mounded ruins form an enclosed area to the west of the church.[1]

FIGURE 16.1. Remnant of a corner, adobe wall in ruins (WACC).

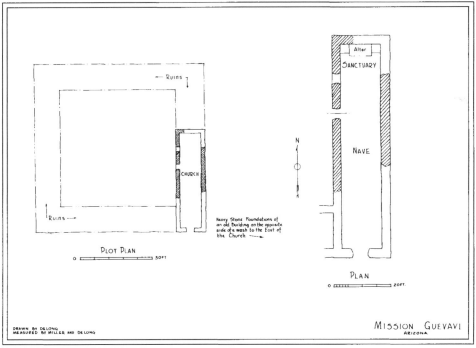

FIGURE 16.1. Plan and plot plan.

FIGURE 17.1. Air view from the southwest (Manley photo).

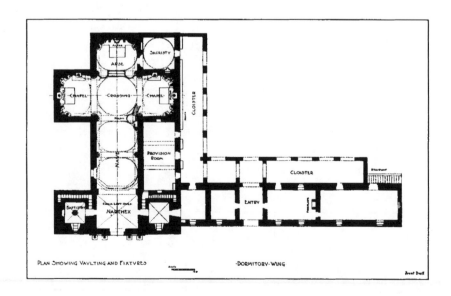

FIGURE 17.2. Plan, by Duell, showing vaulting and dormitory wing (AHS).

CHAPTER SEVENTEEN

San Xavier del Bac
(in Arizona)

Outline Description

ORIENTATION	South.
CONDITION OF CHURCH	Best preserved of the missions, and the only mission church still in use.
FOUNDATIONS	Rubble stone, well cemented.
WALLS	Burned brick with molded brick cornice.
CEILINGS	Nave—flat domes between transverse brick ribs. Dome over crossing supported on a high octagonal drum.
EXTERIOR	Finish—whitewashed plaster. Entrance facade highly decorative with pilasters and panels decorated with low plaster relief.
INTERIOR	Finish—lime plaster with elaborately decorated chapels and reredos. Whole interior embellished with painted decorations and sculpture on walls, ceilings, and cornice.[1,2]

FIGURE 17.I. Decoration over the baptistry door to the nave.

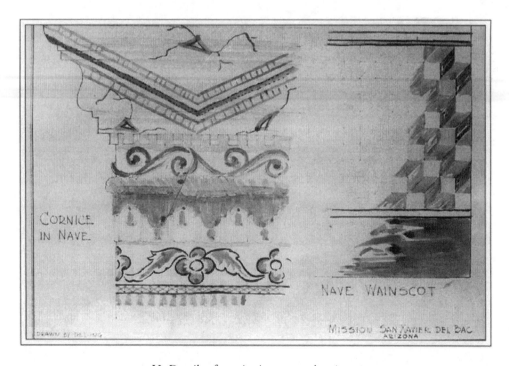

FIGURE 17.II. Details of cornice in nave and wainscot.

CHAPTER EIGHTEEN

Summary and Recommendations

This report shows that whereas the architectural remains of the Sonora mission chain undoubtedly will be of value in making intimate studies of Tumacacori mission—whether for restoration of certain units or in building a complete model of the same—the cultural objects necessary for an exposition of mission life in the seventeenth and eighteenth centuries are lacking. Except for those listed at San Ignacio, Pitiquito, and Tubutama, we found none that was authentic. There are many archaeological sites in the vicinity of the missions, easily reached and worth studying. These should be considered in connection with the background of the missions.

From all available information it would seem that if more definite data are to be obtained on the material culture of the Spanish period of the seventeenth and eighteenth centuries, it will be necessary to make a trip to the valley of Mexico where collections of furniture, clothing, arms, household utensils, horse trappings, etc., are preserved in the Museo Nacional, and in the cities adjacent to the capital. The archives in the city of Mexico conserve documents, plans, pictures, etc., pertaining to the periods mentioned. Such a study, if well done, would not only provide information for the Tumacacori museum studies, but also aid in developing the Spanish-Mexican background of future museums and exhibits in New Mexico, Texas, Missouri, Louisiana, and California.

Considering all phases of the preparation of museum exhibits for any of the foregoing states, the following subjects must be studied in order that accurate historical reconstructions be made in pictures, maps, dioramas, replicas, or identification of original specimens found on the ground:

(a) costumes

(b) household utensils and tools

(c) arms

(d) horses and horse trappings

(e) ranches and ranch life

(f) contemporary accounts, oil paintings

(g) sketches, journals, etc.

(h) maps, charts, and plans

Likewise, a consideration should be given to cultural material of Spanish America now in certain California and New Mexico collections. It must always be borne in mind that when dealing with the various phases of Spain in America, particularly in the Southwest, it is not necessary to consider only the items of Spanish manufacture found in that particular region as being the sole criteria upon which to base reconstruction of the life of the people. We must go further than that. The cultural level of the Spanish frontier was about equal; that is, this holds true as far as the costumes, arms, certain portions of horse trappings, tableware, household utensils, etc., are concerned. There are differences in furniture. For example, seventeenth-century styles of Spanish American furniture stayed among the Rio Grande settlements, while the late-eighteenth-century settlements in California and Arizona were not affected. On the other hand, judging by documentary evidence as well as the actual physical remains, the use of glazed wares known as "majolica" and "Talavera"—made in Puebla, Mexico—were commonly used by the inhabitants of Sonora, particularly at the missions, as well as on the tables of the padres in the California chain and along the Rio Grande. Consequently, a study of the output of the Puebla majolica factories of the seventeenth and eighteenth centuries should provide an excellent cross section of the types of the glazed wares used in Sonora, Arizona, New Mexico, and California.[1]

I cite these items as examples of types of studies that should be carried out on the ground in the valley of Mexico; in the city of Puebla, Mexico; in Querétaro, headquarters of the Franciscan missions; and elsewhere in Mexico, before any intelligent or adequate historical representations of Spanish-Mexican frontier life can be made.

ARTHUR WOODWARD

The characteristic features, materials, construction, and details of the Sonora missions, as they relate to Tumacacori, have been established. Sufficient evidence has been compiled to justify definite architectural study of the Tumacacori problems of stabilization, restoration, and reconstruction. There are also enough data to allow the museum technicians to carry on the architectural portion of the proposed museum exhibits relating to the Franciscan structure.

Walter G. Attwell, Associate Engineer, National Park Service, in his report "Proposed Ruins Stabilization, Mission San José de Tumacácori" (May 1935), has thoroughly outlined the stabilization problems. The work of this character already done by Frank Pinkley, Superintendent of Southwestern Monuments, is highly valuable, but further stabilization as outlined above is also much needed.

It is here recommended that *any work of restoration be kept to a minimum* [emphasis added]. With the architectural data in this report, and with the mission photographs taken by George Grant, any further work can easily follow the character of related work in the existing Sonora missions.

The floors throughout Tumacacori should be restored using burned brick laid in pattern, so common in the other Franciscan structures of this region. With proper study of old photographs and existing conditions at the mission, it might be possible to restore the choir loft.

The outlying buildings at Tumacacori could be reconstructed with some degree of accuracy as to the character of the buildings of this period, but any attempt at authentic restoration would not be successful with the small amount of data available after the excavations of 1934.

In his report "San José de Tumacácori," J. H. Tovrea (January 1936)[2] recommends that detailed measured drawings of Tumacacori be made, recording the restored portions of the church and adjoining structures. He also recommends that the existing painted designs be recorded in detail. These records are of vital importance, as Mr. Tovrea points out, and should be made as soon as possible.[3]

Architectural studies in Sonora of a more accurate nature would prove profitable but are not deemed necessary at this time. As the architectural work connected with Tumacacori progresses, any further data that might be found essential and not covered in this report could easily be obtained in Sonora by one or two men familiar with these missions.

No authentic information regarding the first early structures erected at the mission sites has been obtained. Data on these structures together with details of the processes and methods employed in the erection of Jesuit churches might be obtained at the Museo Nacional in the city of Mexico, where plans, pictures, and Spanish documents are available for study.

Published works relating to the architectural features of the Mexican missions will be found useful to architects and museum technicians. *The Architect and Engineer*, published in San Francisco, contains articles in the July, September, and December issues of 1921, by Prentice Duell, entitled "The Arizona-Sonora Chain of Missions." By the same author is the book *Mission Architecture* (1919), which contains more detailed descriptions of the Sonora missions. *Spanish Colonial Architecture in Mexico* (1901), by Sylvester Baxter, offers splendid data concerning the architectural influence and styles in Mexico.[4,5]

SCOFIELD DELONG AND LEFFLER B. MILLER

Biographical Data and Notes on the Authors, Photographer, and Other Members of the Expedition Team

Scofield DeLong (1903–ca. 1965)

Scofield DeLong was born in Omaha, Nebraska, and was graduated from that city's Central High School in June 1921. He attended the College of Architecture at Cornell University in Ithaca, N.Y., from September 1921 to February 1926, and was elected to Gargoyle, an honorary society in architecture. His internship—practical experience, training as an architect—began in February 1926 in New York City with the architectural firm of L. P. Ward. Between then and August 1934 he had four additional employers: Hobart Upjohn in New York City, S. W. Winburn in Salt Lake City, Masten & Hurd in San Francisco, and the U.S. National Park Service (NPS), with whom he did two stints, four months in 1928 and from September 1933 to August 1934.

On 15 September 1934, he satisfied the requirements and passed the examination before the California State Board of Architectural Examiners and was certified to practice architecture. Living in Berkeley at the time, he continued his employment as Associate Architect, Branch of Plans and Design, NPS, San Francisco.

Assigned to the Sonoran field research project in 1935, DeLong was elected chief of his six-man party of professionals by its members, and with Miller, his fellow architect, was responsible for the measured drawings, data sheets, and part of the text.

After the reports were completed and mimeographed in 1937, DeLong was chosen by the NPS to design and make working drawings for the combination museum–visitor center–office building at Tumacacori. This involved incorporating many of the elements selected from various Sonoran mission churches. His drawings, including some full-size details, are conserved in the NPS Denver Service Center.

DeLong served as Chief Architect in the Western Division, NPS, until 1947. After leaving the NPS, he returned to the practice of architecture in Berkeley, and in 1956 he joined the Northern California Chapter of the American Institute of Architects (AIA). About 1963, he moved to Burlingame, California, and opened his own office, first as DeLong, Zahm Associates, Inc. Some of his principal works, in addition to the Tumacacori visitors' center, included Park Towers Senior Citizens' Retirement Residence; the Elmwood Convalescence Hospital in Berkeley; the visitors' center at Lake Mead National Recreation Area, Nevada; the Pilgrim Plaza Retirement Home in San Mateo, California; and the Turlock, California police and court building. The latter two projects brought him honor awards for excellence in design.[1] There is no reason to assume that in his private practice DeLong departed from his design attitude as exemplified in the 1935 report (see "Authors' Introductions," nn. 15, 19).

Leffler Bequette Miller (1895–ca. 1978)

Leffler Miller was born in Bakersfield, California. He followed the usual path in preparation for the profession of architecture by completing academic studies before he began the practical architectural training required for state registration. Miller was admitted to the University of California in August 1914. He received the A.B. with honors in Architecture, May 1918. He trained for a total of two years and two months in two prominent San Francisco architectural offices before serving for a year and a half as chief designer in the Division of Architecture of the State of California in its Sacramento Office. In 1923 Miller passed his state examination and received his certificate to practice architecture. He joined the Northern California Chapter of the AIA, and was living in Berkeley when he was recruited for the Sonoran expedition in 1935. His title in the NPS was Associate Architect, Field Division of Education.

In addition to the normal duties as a member of the recording team, Miller seems to have done most of the original color sketches, as well as the hand-held camera work that aided in editing the final drawings. After completion of his assignment with the NPS, Miller returned to architectural practice in Berkeley.

Miller received high praise as a sensitive designer from his employers. Also, we have samples of his drawings, many in color, from 1935. Lacking evidence from public records, we must assume that Miller, unlike DeLong, preferred to limit his practice of architecture to residential and small buildings, probably from a one-man office, as was common in Berkeley. He did not respond to questionnaires from professional organizations, like the AIA. Perhaps it is significant that Miller's professional address from about 1956 until about 1977, remained the same: 7 East Parnassus Court.[2] As with DeLong, Miller's attitude toward design is expressed in his drawings and commentary (see "Authors' Introductions," nn. 15, 19).

Albert Arthur Woodward (1898–1986)

Through the courtesy of his friend, Barbara Tyler, here are presented the pertinent parts of Woodward's extraordinary autobiographical notes:

I was born in Des Moines, Iowa, and came to California with my parents in the fall of 1907. We settled in a little hill town, Ramona, in San Diego County. Here I was fortunate enough to be in on the tag end of an era that closed the Old West. We were 14 miles from the end of a small railroad that ran from San Diego to Foster's Station. A six-horse stage of the mud-wagon type met the trains and carried the passengers into the back country as far as Warner's Ranch and Julian. Huge freight wagons brought our food and other daily necessities up the Mussey grade now covered by water of the San Vicente Dam.

It was a time when the automobile had not yet penetrated that country. Everyone traveled by buggy, buckboard or wagon, or on horseback. The Mesa Grande Indian Reservation was only about 15 miles distant. During the summer months the Indians traveled from fiesta to fiesta on the various reservations, always in light "Studebaker wagons" or on horseback. They camped alongside the roads (as did everyone who was caught overnight on the road between towns). Thus, as a youngster I became acquainted with Indians. When I went hunting I found scraps of pottery, arrowheads, manos, and metates, and these items whetted my appetite for more information concerning the people who made them.

My paternal grandfather, Simon Barker Woodward, had formerly been a sergeant in the Seventh Iowa Cavalry and served on the Plains against the Indians during the Civil War. He was along the valley of the Platte River and spent most of the time at Ft. Laramie, Wyoming, one of the most famous posts in the military history of the West. He told me of the Indians.

In 1918 I enlisted in the Twentieth Regular Infantry, Company B. I had left California in the winter of 1917 and had gone back to Des Moines where I obtained a position as car check for the Des Moines Union Railway. About twenty years previously my father had gone to work for this company. I enlisted from Des Moines. After spending time in Ft. Logan, Colorado; Ft. Douglas, Utah; Camp Funston, Kansas; and Ft. Brady, Michigan, I was finally discharged at the Presidio, San Francisco, in 1919.

I returned home and went on a couple of cattle drives; I drove chuck wagon and cooked on one of these and rode on the drag in another.

Later I went to the University of California at Berkeley [1920–1922] where I studied anthropology under Professor A. L. Kroeber and history under Dr. Herbert E. Bolton. Unfortunately, I never finished my university career because when the time approached to return to my junior year's classes, I was 3,000 miles away in New York City where, during the summer vacation, I was working as a reporter, first on the *Bronx Home News*, then a biweekly, and later as leg man for the *New York Evening Journal*. . . . I had a beat in Harlem and covered the territory north of Ninety-sixth Street—courts, police, and civic affairs. On the side I wrote articles for magazines.

I remained on the Journal staff about three years, then came to Los Angeles and obtained a position at the Los Angeles County Museum as Field Man in Anthropology. This was in 1925. . . . My duties entailed the collection and study of all types of material culture from countries all over the world. I also did actual excavations of archaeological sites.

In January 1926 I accepted a position as research worker on the staff of the Museum of the American Indian, Heye Foundation, New York City. Here I did more research on the native population of North, South, and Central America and familiarized myself with the literature of those areas, as well as the material culture. Being familiar with the Spanish language, I was able to translate from books and manuscripts and thus facilitated the necessary research on material from Latin American countries.

Later, in 1928, I returned to the Los Angeles County Museum where I assumed the duties of Chief Curator of History and Anthropology which position was later changed to Director of History and Anthropology.

My new duties included the direction of a small staff of preparators engaged in the making of historical and ethnological dioramas, the collection of specimens of material culture from all over the world, and the identification and accurate classification of the same. I also organized and took into the field archaeological and ethnological expeditions. During 1929, 1930, 1931, and 1932 I was engaged in field research work in Arizona, Utah, Sonora, and California, as well as related library studies.

In 1934–36 I was on leave of absence from the Museum during which time I was in the employ of the National Park Service, first as Laboratory Research Technician, later as Assistant Chief of the Museum Division and Chief Curator with offices at the laboratory in Berkeley, California. At that time the National Park Service was planning new museums in all parts of the United States. My task was to do the research for the various exhibits, and to direct the activities of a large staff numbering between one hundred and two hundred map makers, model makers, and artists. . . .

During 1935 I was archaeologist-historian and interpreter for a National Park Service expedition party engaged in a study of the Kino mission chain [or circuit] in northern Sonora, Mexico. . . . In June 1936 I was ordered to Washington, D.C., where I acted as Assistant Chief of the Museum Division. I administered to the work in that position until November 1936 when I returned to the Los Angeles County Museum.

After 1936 I was appointed as technical advisor in history and archaeology to the National Park Service, particularly with regard to the restoration of Mission La Purisima near Lompoc, California. . . . I speak, read, and write Spanish fluently. In 1940 I spent most of the summer in Mexico making historical, archaeological, and ethnological studies with a view toward utilizing this information in a "good neighbor" show at the Museum. I have written and published two-hundred-odd articles on subjects pertaining to western history, archaeology, and ethnology. I retired from the County Museum in order to better my research and writing.[3]

In May 1961 the University of Arizona conferred the honorary degree of Doctor of Letters (Litt. D.) on Woodward. The formal citation acknowledged his many contributions to the fields of anthropology and history, noting that:

He occupies a unique position among the archaeologists, ethnologists, and historians of the United States. He is one of the most outstanding American authorities on the identification of aboriginal American Indian artifacts.

In World War II he was assigned to the Office of Strategic Services [where he saw service with Admiral Richard Byrd].

A strong believer in the idea that the disciplines of history and anthropology share similar aims, he has long sought to show what historians and anthropologists might learn from one another. Leading specialists in both fields have been in his debt because of his professional services to them, and because of the emphasis on interdisciplinary study that he has personified. His contribution to knowledge, outlined in some nineteen books and innumerable articles, has been twofold: the learned identification of the material culture of modern civilization, and the successful effort to improve and perfect understanding and communication between anthropologists and historians.

During recent years he has served, to this state's [Arizona's] great advantage, as Museum Consultant to the Arizona Pioneers' Historical Society and as an advisor to the Arizona Historical Sites Project.

Woodward spent his retirement years living in Patagonia, in southern Arizona. Before he died there in 1986, he played a large role in the installation of exhibits in a new museum at Tubac State Park, site of a former Spanish military presidio a short distance north of Tumacacori. His Arizona career came full circle.

George Alexander Grant (1891–1964)

George Grant was born in Sunbury, Pennsylvania, on 4 March 1891. In 1929 he was hired by Horace Albright, Director of the NPS, as that federal agency's first photographer. Albright, according to Grant's biographer, wanted the photographer to provide "a comprehensive documentation of the parks, their surroundings, and subjects relevant to their history and character" (Sawyer 1986, 2).

Grant succeeded admirably in his task via tens of thousands of photographs taken by him. As for his contribution to the 1935 Sonoran expedition, his biographer writes: "Sensitive to the plight of the missions, Grant created a photographic record that is both emotionally compelling and factually objective; his documentation remains among the most important and insightful works on the architecture and history of the missions" (Sawyer 1986, 19).

Grant died on 11 October 1964 from respiratory complications and was buried in a churchyard cemetery at Snow Hill, near Baltimore, Maryland.[4]

Robert H. Rose and J. H. Tovrea

Comparatively little can be said about the other two members of the expedition, Rose the Park Naturalist, and Tovrea the engineer. Both were assigned by "Boss" Pinkley to the project, not only to help in any way possible, but also to represent his views, and personally to report back.

Later, in 1936, Rose spent part of the year in Berkeley where he investigated Bancroft Library records of the Kino missions. Some of the results of these endeavors, such as translations of parts of documents—including the 1772 report of Bishop Antonio María de los Reyes—and summaries of information gleaned from mission registers, were reproduced in Pinkley's mimeographed *Southwestern Monthly Report* series (Rose 1936). To Bancroft Library he donated his own personal collection of 139 photos that he made in 1934, and on the 1935 expedition. All were carefully catalogued, each print dated and described in detail.

Tovrea, an engineer on Pinkley's staff, was expected to concentrate on whatever could be found among the Sonoran missions that would relate to Tumacacori, "in the way of restoring in picture form some of her lost details."

Tovrea was not trained as an architect, archaeologist, or art historian, but he performed the kind of research which today would demand the expertise of each of these special fields. He presented his rough sketches of the pulpit at San Ignacio compared with his own pulpit-and-side-altar restoration for the church at Tumacacori. He outlined his rationale for each sketch and also for the debatable choir-loft restoration. All this he did with Pinkley's tacit sanction and possible input. Their conclusions were frequently published as a collaboration.[5]

Tovrea offered an analysis of the results of the 1934 archaeological excavations carried out under the supervision of the NPS professional archaeologist, Paul Beaubien.[6] He even presented arguments pro and con about the original floor plan of Tumacacori, and the padres' intention to use a barrel-vaulted roof. Here he demonstrated his knowledge of theoretical engineering statics by drawing a sectional stress diagram of the conjectural vaulted roof and a two-story bell tower (see Fig. B.5, below). Tovrea's original 1936 "Report on Mission San José de Tumacácori" is a twenty-two-page typescript with nine plates. For details of this remarkable document for a restoration based on research in Sonora, see the summary of Tovrea's report in appendix B, pp. 157–162. Perhaps because of this work, both Woodward and the architects could omit any such conjectures that could be contentious or embarrassing to "Boss" Pinkley.

Pertinent Tumacacori Documents

The 1935 field expedition was officially entitled "The Tumacacori Mission Research Project" for one simple reason: even though the principal subjects of the
reports were twelve missions in Sonora, they were all parts of Father Kino's
original circuit. The subjects were selected for study because of certain family
resemblances to Mission Tumacacori. This National Monument (now a National
Historical Park) was established in 1908. However, it was not often visited, and
except to a few citizens of this region it was not well known. Its historical significance needed to be explained and interpreted. Throughout the 1936 Sonoran
reports Tumacacori is often mentioned.

The purpose of the project was to provide accurate architectural data in order
to make possible the authentic design and construction of a new museum–visitor
center–office building at the Tumacacori National Monument in Arizona. Further, this research venture into Sonora was also intended to improve our understanding of the historical relationship between all the missions of Father Kino's
original circuit. The authors of the 1936 reports on the expedition included a few
illustrations of the Arizona mission at Tumacacori only to show general rele-
vancy; they made no attempt to describe or explain details (see the frontispiece,
and Figs. 1.3, 1.4, and 1.5).

As explained in the Editor's Introduction, for the benefit of readers who may
not be familiar with Tumacacori National Historical Park, it is appropriate to
append here a very brief selection of early illustrations and data about its present
physical status. For some readers it may be helpful to make available the basis for
comparisons with the Sonoran missions that are under review, and to underline
the reasons for the project.

The Piman Indian village of Tumacácori was located on the east bank of Río
Santa Cruz in that part of northern Sonora, Mexico, called Pimería Alta when

Padre Kino founded a mission there in the late seventeenth century as a part of his circuit. For reasons of health and safety—to be nearer to the new Tubac presidio—the mission village was moved about 1753 from the east to the west bank of the river where it still exists, just a few miles north of the present Mexican border.

Because of this 1854 boundary line, many visitors at the National Historical Park, even today, may not recognize the proximity and close ties that bind the missions of northern Sonora to the ruins at Tumacacori, and to the active and far more famous mission church, San Xavier del Bac, a few miles farther north, nearer to the present city of Tucson.

Fig. B.2 is reproduced here, perhaps for the first time, historically because of its early date and for comparison with missions in Sonora, as well as with Duell's plan of San Xavier del Bac (see Fig. 17.2, above). For other reasons which need to be explained, the drawing may also be relevant to the genesis of the renowned Historic American Buildings Survey (HABS), started under the New Deal in 1933 to employ out-of-work architects. This program has been continued by NPS in later years utilizing professional students under faculty advisors during the summer. The HABS collection of drawings and photographs is preserved at the Library of Congress, Washington, D.C.

This measured plan of Tumacacori has extraordinary significance. It is evidence of the very early interest in the architecture of the mission shown by Prentice Duell, together with his architect employer, and a few of his faculty advisors at the University of Arizona. They were all concerned about the rapid deterioration of the old mission, and took the best possible means of recording its church plan for possible future use—either for restoration or reconstruction, and for study and comparison in case the ruins disintegrated.

Duell, it must be remembered, was then working on his 1917 M.A. thesis, published in 1919, *Mission Architecture as Exemplified in San Xavier del Bac*. He realized the historical architectural relationship of his "First placed of all [U.S.] mission churches," San Xavier, to its smaller sister in ruins at Tumacacori.

Nothing yet has come to light at the Arizona Historical Society, or the University of Arizona archives that would reveal the existence of customary notes that normally would have been made during the recording of measurements by those professionals who were listed as helping Duell. But such a careful drawing is evidence enough to suggest that some written documentation might have accompanied this significant recording. Furthermore, there remains a mystery as to how this floor plan of Tumacacori found its way into the office files of the Chief Engineer, NPS, San Francisco, California, where this tracing was made in 1934.

Afterward, Duell joined the American Expeditionary Forces in 1917, later went to teach at the University of Illinois, thence to Harvard, etc., and did not return to Tucson except for visits until 1952, when he came through on his way

FIGURE B.I. Early photograph (ca. 1890) showing the ruins of adobe buildings that once adjoined the mission church on the east (Photo by William Bolton, Dobie Graphics). From facing page 5, "Annual Report, Archeological and Conservation Programs of the Western Region, National Park Service, 1982," Western Archeological and Conservation Center (WACC), Tucson, Arizona. "This report features Tumacacori National Monument with whom our [WACC's] relationship is so closely intermeshed" (from the preface).

to see the Sonoran missions again (this information is gleaned from Duell's papers at the Library of Congress).

As far as we can determine from NPS sources, Duell's 1917 drawing has not been previously published. Because of its location in the NPS files at the San Francisco office along with other drawings of missions published by Duell, there is ample reason to believe that it could have been the genesis of the HABS idea that began some sixteen years later as a means of saving historic buildings by providing emergency relief employment—jobs for architects—an idea that originated with Thomas C. Vint and his staff at the San Francisco Headquarters of NPS.

Since 1928 Vint had been head of general planning for the architectural and landscape program of the Western Field Headquarters for NPS. His office was directly involved with Tumacacori, and had employed DeLong as early as 1928. Vint's Headquarters was moved to Washington, D.C., in 1933. This was precisely the time and place when and where the HABS was activated (see Peterson 1957).

The Tovrea Report–A Summary

Prior to the 1935 expedition, Frank Pinkley, General Superintendent of the NPS Southwestern Monuments Group, and his staff were well aware of the controversial aspects of presenting guesswork and conjectures to the public. At the same time they also felt the daily need to answer questions from visitors, whose curiosity was whetted when they walked through the stabilized ruins and viewed the unfinished bell tower at the National Monument. Something more was needed to satisfy visitors as they vaguely tried to visualize what the original mission might have been, or was intended to be when completed.

Also, those in charge of interpreting the Tumacacori Monument felt the urgency to present their research visually in their annual reports to U.S. officials

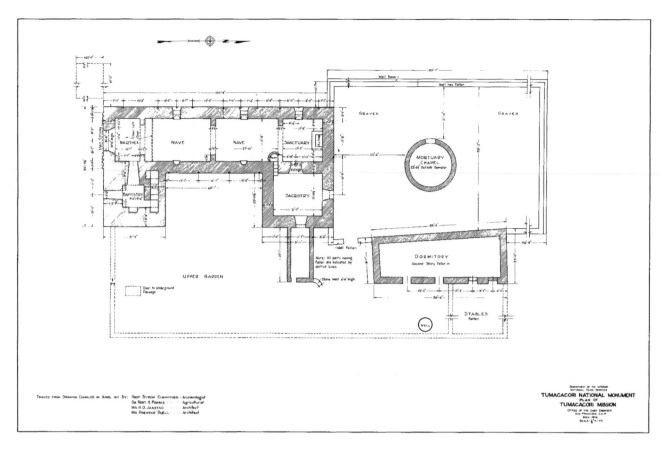

FIGURE B.2. Plan of Tumacacori Mission Church, "traced from drawing compiled in April 1917 [from measurements recorded] by: Prof. Byron Cummings, Archaeologist, and Dr. Robert H. Forbes, Agriculturist [both from the University of Arizona]; and Mr. H. O. Jaastad, [Tucson] Architect, and [the employer of] Prentice Duell, [student] Architect" (Print from NPS, Denver Service Center). See "Authors' Introductions," n. 6.

whenever they might request additional funding. The Tovrea Report "in pictorial form" was part of the answer, i.e., for their best conjectural, exploratory study of Mission Tumacacori substantiated by research in Sonora.

J. H. Tovrea was an engineer from the staff of Frank Pinkley. His special assignment as a member of the six-man team in Sonora was to concentrate on whatever could be found among the Sonoran missions that would relate to Tumacacori "in the way of restoring in picture form some of her lost details." In his introduction, Tovrea explains the genesis of his report:

> Some eighteen years ago [ca. 1918], Superintendent Frank Pinkley of the National Park Service started wondering about Tumacacori and set to work putting pieces of the [unfinished church] puzzle together. His job was harder than ours because he had to start at the beginning. Now, with some parts of the problem solved, it is easier for us to work out other parts. Some of the answers to various parts of Tumacacori's problem, outlined in this report, are accompanied with substantial and logical proof. Others are based on comparative observations of the other missions in the [same Kino circuit]; and still others can be boiled down to the very best and latest guess.

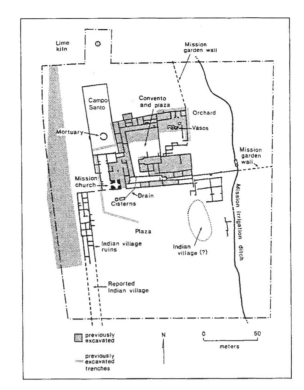

FIGURE B.3. Mission site plan within the original Monument boundaries showing areas of Beaubien's excavations (1934–35). (Fratt 1986, 49, Fig. 3.4)

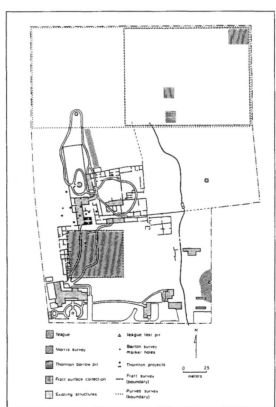

FIGURE B.4. Plan showing expanding boundaries of research at Tumacacori, surface inspections and testing, 1975 to 1981 (Fratt 1986, 62, Fig. 3.11). "An intensive, systematic survey and surface collection of the monument and its surrounding area has not been completed. . . . An adequate survey of the monument's environs would produce a more complete and accurate picture of the mission's extent, data which is lacking at the present" (Fratt 1986, 74).

I found that all the missions in the [circuit] that we visited, were quite radically different from one another with the exception of Caborca, which is practically a twin of Mission San Xavier near Tucson, Arizona [For a discussion of this similarity, see notes to chapter 10, n. 7]. If any one of the missions visited is at all like Tumacacori, it is probably San Ignacio, and it was here that I gathered data which helped to conceive a restoration of Tumacacori's side altars, pulpit, choir loft, rail, and balustrade. It [San Ignacio] also gave me a mental picture of what Tumacacori's interior looked like when it was complete with choir loft and altars. It verified in my mind Superintendent Pinkley's idea that by restoring Tumacacori's choir loft, illusions of greater height and size of the nave would be created and the entire picture would be more in keeping with what the builders meant it to be. . . .

The missions as a whole made me feel that since the buildings were designed to impart a feeling of mystery and sanctity, so should such a feeling be re-created in Tumacacori, as nearly as would be practicable. This could be done in part by restoring some of the altars complete to the image in the niche. When the visitor enters San Xavier he tiptoes and whispers, doubly impressed by what he sees. At the present time, the interior of Tumacacori could be mistaken for the interior of an old banquet hall, a fortress, or even a storage room. (Tovrea 1936)

Since the 1930s there has been no official, published critique of Tovrea's speculative report that had been requested by his superior, Superintendent Pinkley. For many reasons the NPS policy generally has discouraged actual reconstruction or restoration projects in favor of stabilization (see views on this question in "Authors' Introductions," n. 1).

As a curious (if neglected) document, Tovrea's report has historical significance; his twenty-two-page typescript is conserved at the NPS, WACC, in Tucson, Arizona. The published version (Tovrea 1936) contains six plates. He and Pinkley also collaborated on articles based largely on Tovrea's studies, "The Tumacacori Choir Loft Problem" (1936a), and "Tumacacori Alcoves or Transepts" (1936b).

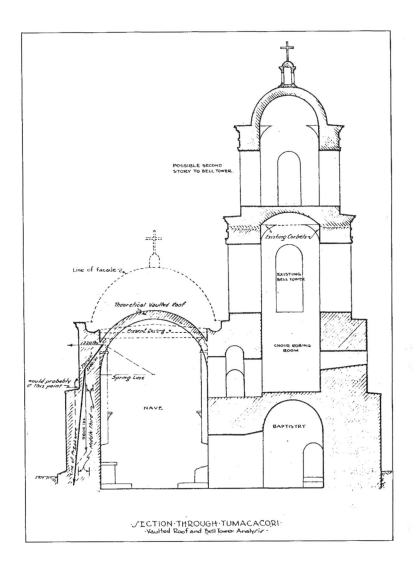

POSSIBLE SECOND
STORY TO BELL TOWER.

Existing Corbels

EXISTING
BELL TOWER

CHOIR ROBING
ROOM

BAPTISTRY

Line of Facade

Theoretical Vaulted Roof

Present Ceiling

Spring Line

NAVE

would probably
if this point

·SECTION·THROUGH·TUMACACORI·
·Vaulted Roof and Bell Tower Analysis·

FIGURE B.5. Section Through Tumacacori, Vaulted Roof and Bell Tower Analysis, drawing by J. H. Tovrea. (Tovrea 1936,
Plate 5)

FIGURE B.6. Tumacacori Restored, a conjectural restoration with two-story bell tower, sketch by J. H. Tovrea. (Tovrea 1936, Plate 6)

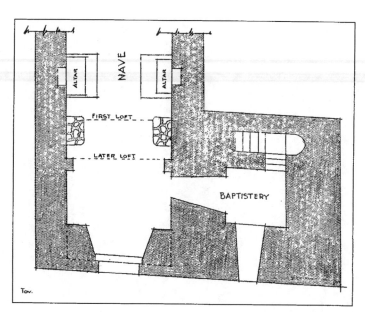

FIGURE B.7. Plan, of church front, showing conjectural restoration of choir loft, by J. H. Tovrea. (Tovrea and Pinkley 1936a, Plate 1)

FIGURE B.8. Theoretical Groin-Vaulted Choir Loft, section showing conjectural restoration, by J. H. Tovrea. (Tovrea and Pinkley 1936a, Plate 3)

Editor's Notes

Editor's Introduction

1. Whiffen 1970, Review of *Paths*, by Roca.

2. Letter to editor, 18 March 1986, from George Kubler.

3. For a discussion of various views, see notes to chapter 1, "Authors' Introductions," n. 13.

4. "Chain" of missions has been a popular expression used by architectural historian Prentice Duell and the authors of this report, no doubt following traditional California usage. Today, many scholars object to its connotation when applied to Kino's Sonora missions. I prefer "circuit" instead of "chain," because, topographically it is more descriptive. Moreover, it connotes a closed loop quality not expressed by such common alternatives as "string" or "group." Too, Father Kino was indeed a frontier "circuit rider."

5. Office Memorandum (longhand) from Russell to Frank Smith, in the archives at the NPS Harpers Ferry Center in Harpers Ferry, West Virginia.

6. From the National Archives, Record Group 79, NPS Classified File, Tumacacori National Monument 501-740.03, Box 2419, Folder 618.

7. As with any historical document, the reader should not hold the authors responsible for the vast amount of factual knowledge published since the manuscript was written more than a half century ago.

Chapter 1. Authors' Introductions

1. In preservation terminology today certain words like "restoration" have taken on a special meaning not always intended in 1935. Since completion of the rebuilding at Williamsburg, Virginia, many who manage historic buildings, including the NPS staff, make sharp distinctions between terms: At Tumacacori their motto is "Preservation *sí*, restoration *no*." The former is interpreted as stabilization and preventive maintenance, the latter as reconstruction. The survey

team in Sonora anticipated possible restoration work at Tumacacori but cautioned that "any [should] be kept to a minimum." For conjectural restoration drawings of the choir loft and bell tower see appendix B, Figs. B.6 and B.8.

2. See Editor's Introduction and chapter 5.

3. Here at the start Woodward states the agreed limits of his area of expertise, but also warns of his tendency, on occasion, to go beyond his assignment. Because of his perceptively different point of view from that of his architect coauthors, his archaeologist's version is helpful.

4. As one might expect, since 1936, the archival religious material on the Franciscan occupation of the missions has attracted the dedicated interest of many scholars (Kessell 1976; Matson and Fontana 1977; McCarty 1981). In these, however, architecture seldom surfaces.

Apparently, the 1933 publication *Los Franciscanos*, by the Mexican scholar, Fernando Ocaranza, was not yet available to Woodward at the Bancroft Library; later, he added it to his reference list (Woodward 1983, 136).

5. It seems curious that Woodward's 1936 statement regarding the scarcity of historical information about the planning or the construction of the missions proper, for the most part is still valid today. The same documents that have given so much concerning the religious and military aspects are strangely silent about the physical nature of the missions. See one notable exception, McCarty 1976a, 65–71.

6. Woodward correctly evaluates the work of Prentice Duell, the University of Arizona graduate student architect, and Francis C. Lockwood, the English professor. He was kind enough not to mention that the teacher depended on the student almost entirely for the architectural descriptions in his book. We have included several of Duell's (1921) drawings to illustrate certain details in Woodward's text not otherwise covered.

The fascinating career of Prentice Duell (1894–1960) deserves further study (He was a balloon pilot-observer, American Expeditionary Forces, WWI). After many years as a productive research fellow in Egyptian and Etruscan art at the Fogg Art Museum, Harvard University, Duell was archaeologist at Colonial Williamsburg and in 1953 revisited his first love—the missions of northern Sonora. Indeed, he planned to write a book about them. The Library of Congress, Division of Prints and Photographs, preserves his notes, map, negatives, and related papers (L.C. 9273–9283).

7. Woodward, as archaeologist, was fascinated with these stone "breastworks"—trincheras in Sonora—stimulated no doubt by the published research of Sauer and Brand (1931). There have been many excavations at trincheras sites since then—with reports (Hinton 1955; Johnson 1963–64; McGuire 1984; McGuire and Villalpando 1989) confirming the prehistoric culture—and yet none has turned up significant evidence relating to the Indians of the Spanish mission era that goes beyond the brief descriptions by the eighteenth-century

Jesuit missionaries (Nentwig 1764; Pfefferkorn 1795). One investigator (Johnson 1963–64, 182) cited Woodward's article on the La Playa site.

8. Woodward's source for Pima-Papago tribal names was F. W. Hodge's then authoritative *Handbook*, published in 1907–10. However, he also gives us his own firsthand account of the vernacular coinage for the term "Cojate," which certain Pima-Papago Indians called themselves (see Fontana 1987, 150–54). Woodward's last few paragraphs on ethnology and etymology have upset some, but when carefully read, remind us that—being a humanist writer, as well as "field" historian—when skeptical of academic findings, he occasionally enlivens his text by having a bit of fun with his Ph.D. colleagues, as he does with this tongue-in-cheek digression.

He reverts from the role of straight-faced academic when he cites as "the truth of the matter," i.e. Pima-Papago relationship, first by quoting here from the Pima himself, on "Cojate," and then later giving the linguistic definition from the *Handbook*. He must have approved of the looser version by Dr. Polzer (Woodward 1983, 8–9), "The derivation of segments in the name [Papagos] indicates that they were the 'people in the sand desert who ate beans'." Others, put off by such levity, correct him: "Wrong!" they protest, "We simply don't know."

9. For a more academic and recent etymological treatment of these terms, see Fontana 1983.

10. See Woodward 1936b.

11. Research in Washington, D.C., archives reveals that Grant's negatives made on the Sonoran expedition were fortuitously preserved at the U.S. Interior Department, not because of their subject matter, but rather because of the reputation of George Alexander Grant. He was the National Park Service's first "official," i.e. master, professional photographer (see Grant biography, Sawyer 1986).

Another point should be noted here: by "architectural photographs herein," the author probably refers to certain detailed views—hand-held camera shots—taken by Miller (primarily to supplement the measured drawings), rather than to the general views by Grant, who used a tripod, and special lenses, as well as 5″ x 7″ film.

12. The probable source for this "prevailing local myth" was Duell (1921, pt. 1 (July), 75). His thesis on San Xavier was written at the University of Arizona in 1917. However, the later biographer of San Xavier, Dr. Bernard Fontana, at the same university, rejects the idea as, "preposterous . . . There are fine building stones less than a mile away . . . and there is absolutely nothing in the documentary record to suggest that women had to carry the stones . . . The stones were almost certainly carried by mules or horses; the Spaniards and Indians had plenty of them" (Fontana, note to editor, 1988). See another local myth disclaimer in note 17 below.

13. Here the authors identify one of the most intriguing mysteries yet unsolved in southwestern mission research: How did lonely friars do it?, i.e., construct

frontier buildings that still delight the eye and impress the contemplative mind. For Sonora, at least, we still need more research.

In chapter 4 (Cocóspera) Woodward digs out and quotes, in architectural terms, the best of Kino's writings (1683–1711) on this elusive subject, i.e. details of actual design and construction. He notes that sometimes these juicy bits have been omitted "as probably too mundane." A few exceptions prove the rule (Burrus 1971, 277; Pfefferkorn 1949, 79–81).

Schroeder (1957, 12–14) cites evidence that at least some buildings from Padre Kino's time and place were constructed by Indians without Spanish help as has been frequently assumed.

Dr. Mardith Schuetz-Miller has researched the master masons et al., who worked on mission churches of San Antonio, Texas (1983). Also, in 1987, she translated and edited "Architectural Practice in Mexico City" [1794–1813]. She maintains: It is a myth that missionaries acted as their own architects and builders, except in some cases, for the first temporary churches. But when it came to building permanent churches, they recruited professionals from Central Mexico (see Kubler 1944).

For Texas, Dr. Schuetz-Miller has identified the names of about 75 artisans connected with the building trade up to 1823, and she is currently working out the career profiles of another 154 in California up to 1850, mostly Spaniards and Indians trained under them. Thus far, Dr. Schuetz-Miller has not yet cited evidence concerning master-masons and carpenters (at Cocóspera, Tubutama, Pitiquito, Oquitoa, or San Ignacio) on the Sonoran frontier; but she believes that they will someday get recognition for what they built. Professional architects applaud her. Only too well do they understand the need for historians to identify those who actually do plan and design buildings. So frequently, they simply give credit to the client or administrator (see notes to chapter 13, n. 7).

In New Mexico, James Ivey has completed a meticulous NPS historic structures report (Ivey 1988) on excavations to show individual seventeenth-century friars' roles (with chronology in design and construction), for three stone churches of the Salinas National Monument (Abó, Quarai, and Humanos).

14. Architecture, we may need to be reminded, was recommended highly for use in the late-sixteenth-century memory-training courses (mnemonics) for Jesuit novitiates in northern Italian cities as well as Rome and possibly elsewhere: "The student should practice creating dramatic images of various kinds, and designing locations for them: palatial buildings or spacious churches would be among the best" (Spence 1984, 5).

15. In this authors' summary of the historical styles, we find one of the few reminders of their 1930s academic training and the implied method for evaluating, i.e., European pigeonholing, of Latin American art (Kelemen 1967, 1:vii–viii). Since 1936, half a century of published research on Mexican art and architecture enables us now to study this portion of the authors' report with full

awareness of the time gap (see Kubler 1985). As the authors candidly admit, their academic exercise—providing a brief, historical "handbook" summary of architectural styles—was then considered a mandatory introduction to their subject.

But today such a review, however helpful in urban centers, seems far less relevant, even misleading when used to evaluate frontier mission architecture. Nevertheless, it is important for us to include this exercise as part of a 1936 document. It serves to remind us how confusing it has been to rely upon the array of European styles in order to understand design in Sonoran missions, i.e., the material forms which the authors have so sensitively and reverently recorded in their drawings, photographs, and written descriptions (Weismann 1985, 195).

16. On painting by Indians see discussion, notes to chapter 13 (Tubutama), n. 7.

17. Historians at San Xavier have admitted that they have yet to discover any reliable evidence in photographs or drawings that would confirm the statement that the white dome of San Xavier was ever painted to imitate tile. Apparently, DeLong and Miller quoted Prentice Duell's passing remark in his article, "The Arizona-Sonora Chain of Missions" (Duell 1921, pt. 1 (July), 65).

18. See notes to chapter 7 (Oquitoa), n. 4, and chapter 11 (Pitiquito), n. 1.

19. Here the authors avoid all reference to the complex framework of historical styles. As architects with discernment, they evaluate the Sonoran missions in terms of time, spirit of place, and the basic forms of architecture.

Chapter 2. The Missions of Sonora and Arizona

1. See notes to Editor's Introduction, n. 4.

2. See Roca 1967, 7–8.

3. Historian Dr. Charles W. Polzer, SJ, recently has pointed out that in all probability Real de San Juan Bautista became the first capital of Sonora ca. 1650, almost certainly after the death of Perea in 1645 (Woodward 1983, 9).

4. Some readers have failed to note that Bolton confided to Woodward, his student, that he (Bolton) had found new evidence, and revised his 1919 printed statement about the location of Kino's burial place. Woodward, in 1935, certainly knew that it was under the old Magdalena capilla and not at San Ignacio, as a careful reading of his text makes clear.

5. "Serapio Dávila *in 1928* . . . opened trenches in front of the present church . . . " (Polzer 1982, 58).

6. The search for the grave of Padre Kino continued in Magdalena from the 1930s until finally in May 1966 an international team (an architect, anthropologists, and historians) located and identified Kino's remains under the (1711) capilla site, only a few hundred feet from the spot under the (1705) Campos church that Sr. Dávila had shown to Woodward. A new fifteen-acre memorial plaza has since been constructed around the grave site.

The momentous discovery was vividly and graphically portrayed by Dr. Polzer (1982, 58–68). We have included the corrected grave site in Woodward's 1935 sketch of Dávila's 1928 excavations (Fig. 2.2). The corrections (site and dates) are based on Dr. Polzer's ingeniously overlaid plans (1982, 62). Woodward correctly reported the best data available at the time. In 1989 one of the participants in the discovery, Jorge Olvera, architect, was preparing for publication a definitive account of the search for Kino's grave, with details not in Dr. Polzer's summary.

It should also be noted here that the pioneering founder of missions, Padre Eusebio Kino, sj (1645–1711), native of Segno (near Trent), Italy, was honored by the United States in 1965; a seven-foot bronze statue was placed in the National Statuary Hall of the Capitol Building in Washington, D.C. Similar statues to honor this heroic international figure were also erected in Hermosillo, Sonora, and in Phoenix and Tucson, Arizona. The tricentennial of Kino's arrival in Sonora was widely celebrated in 1987, both in the U.S. and Mexico.

7. For details of the Franciscan takeover see McCarty 1981.

8. Perhaps because his sources were "hazy" Woodward omitted Cocóspera from this list of missions; we add this mission from more recent references, Roca 1967, 87 and McCarty 1981.

9. Recent scholarship has revealed that the 1772 report of Antonio Reyes (1729–86), was based on secondhand information and is "singularly unreliable." But, as Woodward points out, Reyes had little to say about the mission buildings per se, somewhat more about geographical locations; the Indians' behavior, inclinations, and customs; crops, large or small, poor or not; but mostly about statistics, the census book and temporal goods, such as the internal adornments; and equipment in the sacristy. At best, the report was a checklist, not a description important to Woodward's report.

Chapter 3. San Ignacio de Cabórica

1. We live in an era of awakened interest in historical buildings as icons of our past. Woodward here speaks for an increasingly large segment of the general public who may have been saturated with the "blood and guts" aspect of mission life. Political feuding among friars seems to have become more important to researchers than the *total* function of the mission itself, and of buildings as the visible instruments of a reciprocating, acculturizing process. To Woodward, the Sonoran missions, as artifacts, had much to say.

2. In his *prólogo* to Woodward's Spanish edition, Dr. Polzer comments eloquently on the vandalism of indifference:

> Throughout the text of Woodward's report are frequent references to the damage wrecked by waves of treasure hunters, both Mexican and Norteamericano. This madness will probably never cease, but we should take every occasion to quiet the rumor and proclaim the truth. There has

never been any *hidden* treasure in any of these mission sites. Unscrupulous tricksters have planted small items to encourage the ignorant to invest in even greater frauds. The only treasure lies *open and exposed*: It is the splendor of the buildings and the monuments erected by the sacrifice and hard work of our ancestors who lived in hope. The only disgrace that can befall these monuments is the lack of care and respect we show them, and that lack usually begins with ignorance and grows with greed. (Woodward 1983, 10)

3. Concerning the "Reyes Report of 1772" and Woodward's disclaimer, see notes to chapter 2, n. 9.

4. For reference to Woodward's interest in Trincheras ware, see notes to chapter 1, "Authors' Introductions," n. 7 and related text.

5. See Fontana et al. 1962.

Chapter 4. Nuestra Señora del Pilar y Santiago de Cocóspera

1. Woodward—the exacting historian-archaeologist, himself a meticulous illustrator—was indeed hypercritical of Browne, the artist-reporter who was covering the wild west scene for the popular *Harper's New Monthly Magazine* in the 1860s. Browne's sketches (engraved by others) do convey firsthand impressions and are valuable when used, as here, for comparison. I find Browne's explanation of working in "The Apache Country" quite convincing:

Sketching in Arizona [and Sonora] is a rather ticklish pursuit. I shall not readily forget my experience of the canyons and thickets, and the queer feeling produced by the slightest sound, as I hurriedly committed the outlines to paper . . . An artist with an arrow in his back may be a very picturesque object to contemplate at one's leisure; but I would rather draw him on paper than sit for the portrait myself . . . and if any man of genius and enterprise thinks he can do better under the circumstances he is welcome to try. (Browne, L. 1969, 288–89)

2. Except for the explicit memoirs of Padre Kino himself, scholars continue to find records of the mission at Cocóspera to be sketchy and uncertain. Thus, as Woodward insists, the remains at the site still require careful study and interpretation, especially for critical periods. For a chronology of Cocóspera's history, in Spanish, see Wasley 1976.

3. In these excerpts from Kino's memoirs, Woodward gives us the key to understanding the Padre's high regard for basic architectural elements and their impact on the natives: he speaks like a designer about high and strong walls, good and pleasing arches, and the two chapels which form the transepts, supporting a high cupola [dome] with a sightly lantern above. Among the neighboring Indian tribes the word about such a "heavenly space" at Cocóspera spread to other areas;

no wonder the Indians from far and wide (even Yumas) came with gifts to attend the dedication ceremonies! See also Burrus 1971, 277, text related to n. 56.

4. Prior to the explorations of Kino ca. 1700, many European cartographers showed lower California as an island cut off from land access to the mainland. When the Yuma (Quechan) Indians of southwestern Arizona presented Kino with a gift of certain rare, blue shells that he recognized came only from the Pacific side of "the island," Kino explored the land route and disproved the idea that lower California was an island: "California no es isla, sino península." His map recording the discovery was published in France in 1705, and became the basis for maps of that region until the nineteenth century (Burrus 1965).

5. According to one eminent historian, Woodward's remarks dealing with the interpretation of "burning" or "destruction" of a mission are extremely significant. "Investigation seems clearly to indicate that such occurrences seldom obliterated the original buildings or sites. More often than not the structures were repaired and remodeled at that time. Even the statement that a 'new' church was built does not necessarily imply that the older foundations [or materials] were not employed in the newer construction" (Dr. Charles W. Polzer, sj, in Woodward 1983, 10).

6. The recent investigations of adobe structures at Tumacacori in Arizona (Crosby 1985) substantiate Woodward's view concerning the durability of adobe structures. On page vii of his report, Crosby quotes from D. H. Lawrence, *Mornings in Mexico*: "That they don't crumble is the mystery. That those little, squarish mud heaps endure for centuries after centuries while Greek marble tumbles asunder and cathedrals totter is the wonder. But a single human hand with a bit of new soft mud is quicker than time and defies the centuries."

7. See n. 1, above.

8. As one studies the Cocóspera nave from 1935 photographs and drawings, it seems clear that the design was conceived by a padre or his master mason who had acquired considerable skill from previous building experience. Here, the designer was faced with a unique rehab-structural problem beset with constraints (the existing shell) as well as new requirements. His solution was to construct four huge, oversized niches—as side chapels—recessed between interior buttresses, within the total thickness (about 4′) of the inner wall. Note especially the plan (Fig. 4.5, above).

The space effect of these undulating walls discourages the notion of "neoclassical" influence, and indicates, not the adoption of some European style, but rather the dire necessity to make the constricted nave seem to be wider and yet to gain impressive side chapels. This was not a typical nave treatment, for it required almost double the wall-thickness-to-span ratio. Such thick walls would be extravagant for a new building. This job, it seems, was done by an inspired, well-practiced, "niche specialist."

In considering the resulting spatial effect of the remodeled nave, one finds here a rare example of what Kubler in his monumental study of Mexican architecture describes as the "cryptocollateral" church plan: a single-naved church flanked by lateral chapels (used in the sixteenth century mostly by the Dominicans in Mexico City and Oaxaca).

The Cocóspera treatment is no doubt an unusual coincidence of purpose, i.e., an effort to create the effect of more space when there is very little, and yet to retain the essentials needed by the Franciscans to satisfy their desire for a unified, "primitive simplicity of faith and ceremony . . . rigorously concentrated upon essence rather than upon externalities" (Kubler 1948, 2: 240–41 and 283 ff.).

9. From Nicholas Bleser at Tumacacori (letter December 1986) we learn that this design use of color and texture from crushed burned brick has, indeed, been recorded there, in the same place that Woodward noted. Color slides of this feature were made when they excavated during the stabilization project long after 1935. This remark by Woodward suggests that he had studied thoroughly the (1934) excavations at Tumacacori prior to leaving for the Sonora expedition. Frequently, he notes similarities in unusual bits of mission design and construction.

10. Drainage must have been one of the criteria for mission micro-site selection. "Drains [like those seen at Cocóspera and Tumacacori] were a common feature of Franciscan mission complexes" (Bleser, letter December 1986).

11. The elevated position of the Cocóspera mission church overlooking the valley suggests that Padre Kino may have decided, instead of separate military-type towers, to design the twin octagonal bell towers somewhat higher and to construct them even more solidly than in the normal fortress-church. The architectural forms seem to confirm that the towers could function well for observation and also present a strong defensive appearance.

12. Woodward's regretful departure from Cocóspera suggests that this mission, although in a semi-ruinous condition, impressed him as having more to offer archaeologists than many of the others. Discerning visitors to the site express similar reactions. And these two 1936 NPS manuscript reports have had a more recent influence.

A Spanish translation of Woodward's report was published in Hermosillo, Mexico (Woodward 1983). Since then, there has been a reawakening of interest by the Mexican government, which in 1986 sent a team of scholars—archaeologist, architect, historian, et al.—to report on the Kino circuit of missions, presumably to aid in celebrating the tricentennial of Kino's arrival (1687) in the Pimería Alta. They even discussed the possibility of restoring the church at Cocóspera and were delighted to obtain copies of the architects' measured drawings, which they recognized as an invaluable resource that complemented Woodward's analytical text and Grant's photography (Fontana, letter to editor 5 June 1986).

Since 1935, only one serious article on the architecture has been published in the U.S., and it was concerned only with the church, not the mission site and other buildings (Davis and Goss 1977). By 1977 conditions (access) at the site had changed. The authors depended heavily upon Woodward's text, the measured drawings by DeLong and Miller, and the photographs by Grant, all available from various archives in Tucson.

Their principal contribution was to provide hitherto unknown dates and the name of the administrative priest, Fr. Juan de Santiesteban, OFM, who was in charge of the mission from 1784 to 1801. The church was rebuilt from ca. 1788–96 to 1800. They cited documents showing that Father Santiesteban was curate of the mission during the rebuilding period and gave him credit for the church's completion. The padre's letters mentioned "extensive use of Indians . . . and that skilled laborers (*operarios*) would be moving on once the construction was completed" (see n. 8 above).

Davis and Goss reviewed the history of the church's repeated destruction and reconstruction, quoting in part from Woodward's report. With his help, they explained the unique roof construction, redrafting critical elements selected from the architects' 1935 measured drawings. Also, the authors added an excellent interpretation of Franciscan iconography in the decorative details of Cocóspera's painting and sculpture.

Unfortunately, in their architectural analysis, the authors attempted to relate the design of this remodeled frontier church to the European stylistic framework without evidence of direct connections. Indeed, they depended for guidance on general handbooks, while neglecting important works on traditional architecture such as Kubler 1948.

Chapter 5. *Santa María Magdalena*

1. This date has recently been corrected to 1830–32 (Polzer 1982, 62).

2. For update see Fontana 1981b, 45.

3. Dr. Carl Parcher Russell, Chief, Museum Division within the National Park Service, Branch of Field Research and Education, Berkeley, California ca. 1934–35, author of "The Tumacacori Story."

4. Emiliano Zapata (ca. 1879–1919) was a popular Mexican revolutionary from 1910 to 1919. Plutarco Elías Calles (1877–1945), a native of Sonora, was an agrarian reformist in politics who served as the President of Mexico, 1924–28. His regime was notable for the closing of Catholic churches.

Chapter 6. *Altar*

1. When Father Pfefferkorn was sent to administer Mission Atil in 1756, he was "also assigned the task of administering spiritual aid to the Spanish garrison of Altar and to the Spanish families living in that region" (Pfefferkorn 1949, 261).

2. Two new presidios were established: San Ignacio de Tubac (now Tubac, Arizona)—in 1752 (Kessell 1970, 125–26); and Santa Gertrudis de Altar (now

Altar, Sonora)—in 1755 (Almada 1952, 55). Each was manned by fifty troops and stationed near mission villages (Moorhead 1975, 52).

3. See n. 1 above.

4. On orders of the king, the Marqués de Rubí made an inspection tour of the presidios along the northern frontier of New Spain in 1766–68. He was accompanied by Nicolás de Lafora, Captain of the Engineers, who wrote a remarkable journal, and under whose direction Second Lieutenant Joseph de Urrutia surveyed the sites and drafted the overall map of the area covered, from Texas to the Gulf of California.

Even more remarkable, Urrutia drew the plans (to scale) for some twenty-one individual towns, forts, and their environs. He included buildings, trails, and irrigated fields. The original manuscript plans are conserved in the Map Room of the British Library (ADD. MSS. 17662), but copies exist at Bancroft Library and the Library of Congress. All twenty-one presidio plans were reproduced (Moorhead 1975, 116–57); some were previously analyzed (Gerald 1966, 1968).

5. For current archaeological research on the presidios in Arizona see an interesting series of well-illustrated articles by Jack Williams in *The Smoke Signal* (Williams 1986a, 1986b, 1988).

Chapter 7. San Antonio de Oquitoa

1. Reyes, "Report of 1772," 57.

2. "Available documentary evidence makes it fairly clear (a) that the sun-dried adobe walls of Mission Oquitoa were constructed during the Jesuit period, i.e., before 1767. This hall-shaped church, with its flat roof of mesquite vigas and *carrizo latillas,* would appear to be the only still-standing and still-in-use mission structure of the Jesuit period in the Pimería Alta. Documentary evidence also suggests that (b) the unusual facade was a Franciscan addition, as probably also was the triumphal arch inside" (Fontana, letter to editor, 1988).

3. A careful study of figure 7.2 confirms that, indeed Woodward had a discriminating eye. The original facade of the church at Oquitoa ranks well above most of the other smaller churches in its sophisticated architectural composition, and more than any other, strongly suggests either graphic aid to supplement some padre's long-remembered image, or the possible involvement of a professional architect-master mason. The church deserves further study, as do the nearby tombs.

4. As late as 1980 restoration work [seemingly hasty and careless] was completed at Oquitoa (Polzer 1982, 44). "They uncovered evidences of painted wall decorations not visible before, also that the arch between nave and sanctuary was a later addition. Most of the original wall painting disappeared, apparently without adequate documentation; to date nothing has been published concerning this restoration nor likely ever will be" (Fontana, letter to editor, 15 May 1986).

Chapter 8. San Francisco de Atil

1. Father Soler's predecessor, Ignaz Pfefferkorn, the last Jesuit, related some great experiences concerning his own arrival at Atil in 1756 (see Pfefferkorn 1949, 261–62). However, Pfefferkorn mistakenly attributed the construction there to Kino (memo on Father Pfefferkorn from Fontana to editor, 1990).

2. The sun-dried adobe church of Atil, whose ruins are described here, was built in 1747 by some of 210 Piman Indians recruited by Jesuit missionary Jacobo Sedelmayr from "the coast and Sea of California." His letter of 20 March 1747 appears in translation by Mills (1932, 151) (Fontana, note to editor, 1988).

Chapter 9. Santa Teresa

1. Reyes, "Report of 1772," 56.

2. For a discussion by Woodward of the trincheras see his introduction, pp. 4–5, n. 7, and references.

3. DeLong and Miller's west-northwest orientation, which is based on DeLong's drawing (Fig. 9.I), does not agree with Woodward's southwest orientation which would locate the nave and entrance in the other wing of the L-shaped church.

Chapter 10. Nuestra Señora de la Concepción de Caborca

1. Kino 1919, 1: 130 ff.; Kino 1971, 47–53.

2. Forbes 1952 (American version), and Ruibal Corella 1976 (Mexican version).

3. Letter appears in translation in Mills 1932, 151.

4. Reyes, "Report of 1772," 59.

5. The river apparently changed its course sometime after the church was built. Since 1890, flood damage to the mission church has been documented by Roberto Gaona, a native (and possibly a descendant of the architect?): Parts of the church have fallen four times, a room in August 1890; a large room in January 1899; the back part of the convento and two more rooms closer to the main altar, 1915; and the main altar on 30 July 1917 (letter from Gaona, 12 March 1922, the Prentice Duell Collection, L.C. 9282, 10).

When Duell revisited the Sonoran missions in February 1953, he recorded another method used by natives for documenting flood damage by the gradual falling of the convent arcade: In 1936 there were five arches; by 1943, four; and in 1953 only two remained which he photographed (ibid., L.C. 9279).

Since 1935 when our photographs were made, the Mexican government has restored the east wall, the south transept, and the dome (Roca 1967, 122), not for religious use, but first as a war monument, and later as a general museum with revolving exhibits, lectures, and concerts. The mission had served as a fortress in the defeat of the army of American filibusters headed by Henry Crabb in 1857.

6. " . . . beginning in the 1950s the Mexican government and Sonora State government have combined efforts to restore the entire body of the church at Caborca as well as a portion of the north convento. The entire church is a municipal museum, one displaying artifacts relating to the region's prehistoric and historic Indians as well as to its mission and military history. There is also a changing display of works of local artists" (Fontana, note to editor, 1988).

7. The marked similarity between both facade and plan of the mission church at Caborca and the more famous San Xavier del Bac near Tucson, Arizona, less than 200 miles away, has attracted the curiosity of tourist and scholar alike. In May 1917, Prentice Duell, a twenty-two-year-old graduate student at the University of Arizona, completed the first serious architectural study of San Xavier del Bac. This M.A. thesis was published (Duell 1919). He believed that San Xavier was the most perfect example of mission [church] architecture, and he made meticulous measured drawings to record the building as it was "finished by the Franciscans in 1797." Like many a trail-blazing scholar, Duell felt the need to assume a working premise.

Lacking the resource of later historical studies that provided dates (1803–1809) for the look-alike church at Caborca, Duell felt that surely it must have been built from the same plan, either before or concurrently with San Xavier del Bac, thus serving as the less-perfected prototype. He theorized that the experience at Caborca had enabled the architect of San Xavier to remedy faults of construction and proportion, and to incorporate other refinements which he noted (Duell, l.c. 9282, 2.10).

Also, Duell suggested that an inscription of the name, "PEDRO BOJ[S]. [Bojorquez] AÑO DIE 1797," boldly carved on the wooden door to the sacristy at San Xavier might possibly be the name of the architect or builder, not merely a carpenter or "a manufacturer of wooden doors," as one latter-day historian has proposed (Fontana 1961, 11). Architectural history suggests it is far more likely that architects and builders receive recognition for their work from inscriptions, i.e., cornerstones, etc., than from church records (Duell 1919, 68, 89; Duell 1921, pt. 2 (September), 74–75).

A more recent study (Goss 1975), using documents not available to Duell in 1917, makes a comparative analysis of "five possible explanations for the similarities of the two mission churches which would link their construction and thereby establish kinship." By a process of elimination—based upon both Duell's and DeLong and Miller's drawings—and his own stylistic analysis, Goss concluded: "There can be little question that Nuestra Señora de la Concepción [at Caborca] was a copy of San Xavier" (177), not the other way around, and further that, "Generally, visual evidence coupled with sketchy documentation . . . suggest that, as the construction crews finished at San Xavier about 1779, they may have gone to Caborca and started work there" (177). Duell, although deprived of his pioneering hypothesis, i.e., Caborca as the prototype, would surely have agreed with

Goss, "that the builders of mission Caborca exhibited excellent taste in the choice of San Xavier as their guiding example" (178).

8. Woodward, the archaeologist, who had been quite careful in observing the nuances of color, prefers to use slang rather than current, art-historical terminology in describing his impressions of other decorative details.

9. Such similar bench details discovered in the "Beaubien" excavations at Tumacacori have been accurately recorded in drawings made in 1934. See Attwell 1937.

Chapter 11. San Diego del Pitiquito

1. In the early months of 1967, the use of cleaning detergents to wash the nave walls revealed that "the whole church [interior] had been decorated with large liturgical and doctrinal murals" (Polzer 1982, 44). Thus, to make the dimly lit murals effective, there was need for simplicity and restraint in the design of the pulpit and other plastic forms.

2. A similar triple-scallop head is used prominently above the window in the choir loft at Mission San Xavier del Bac, but the combined masonry steps and seat in the sacristy may be unique to northern Sonora. Father Kieran McCarty, OFM, recalls that he has seen nearly identical window seats in cells of the friars in the Augustinian monastery (ca. 1540–60) at Acolman in the Estado de México. The seat was used by friars to read under the direct light source. The steps provided convenient access to operate the casement window, placed high in the wall, of necessity. Father McCarty points out that light was always a problem in pre-electric churches (Fontana, note to editor, 1988). Such modest, functional details for light and ventilation (material culture) offer clues to the role of both tradition and memory as a possible design source on the frontier.

3. The remains of similar arcade piers (or column bases) along with connecting arches, etc., were photographed at Tumacacori in the 1880s (Arizona Historical Society, copy 1424, "Tumacacori before 1900," photo 11).

Chapter 12. San Juan del Bísanig (San Valentín)

1. Kino refers to this mission as "San Valentín" (Kino 1919, 2: 182). See also Matson and Fontana 1977, 146–47.

2. Part of the information Woodward gives the reader here was gleaned from the notorious "Reyes Report of 1772." But, his finding the large quantity of shells at Bísanig seems to lend the report some credence. However, as elsewhere, Fray Antonio de los Reyes relates little of significance for mission architecture, planning, or construction.

3. Woodward's evocative tribute to the mission at Bísanig goes well beyond a mere scientific, archaeological report and reveals his personal reactions.

4. Woodward's explicit directions—however valid for 1935—today are obsolete; roads and ranch ownerships change. But mission guidebooks and tours

still omit Bísanig. In the meantime, we have Woodward's site plan and his epigraphic "benediction," written while he was observing the physical remains of Mission San Valentín.

Chapter 13. San Pedro y San Pablo de Tubutama

1. A dam, the Presa Cuauhtémoc, which was built below Tubutama on the Río Altar between 1947 and 1950, has flooded most of Tubutama's former farm lands (Fontana, notes to editor, 1988, 1990).

2. Polzer 1982, 43.

3. Roca 1967, 103–4.

4. Kino 1919, 1: 140 ff.

5. Kino 1971; Kessell 1976, 94–98.

6. Cullimore 1954, 13–22.

7. Here, we need to make several major points concerning Woodward's 1936 comment about the painted motifs on the nave cornice. Perhaps today he might more accurately have written that the effect of Pima-like designs painted over the simplified entablature might seem "bizarre" to anyone expecting to find "academic good taste." Tour guides still speculate that "the designs are crude attempts to emulate marble—diamonds and ovals with little legs coming out of them—certainly whimsical and charming," but we add, hardly convincing.

Today, it may be possible to find meaning (not whimsy) in this overlay of native designs—painted on the classical, *cyma recta* molding atop the nave cornice (Figs. 13.4 and 13.III). Are they not a highly visible *metaphor*, the Franciscan teacher being "willingly Indianized" by his apt and motivated neophyte? We know that the padres encouraged Indian participation in the labor of construction; why not also in the actual design and execution of final forms within the church?

One local specialist in Papago pottery rejects this interpretation as "not only speculative but highly questionable." He objects on the grounds that "Papago pottery was essentially plain and they lacked any tradition of painting other than the simplest of design, as on hide shields and on their bodies." But the mission church was architecture, not pottery; the work was done under the supervision of padres or their surrogates who have long regarded impressive church buildings as essential to the "spiritual conquest."

At Tubutama, Fray Francisco Antonio Barbastro was well known as a minister sympathetic to the goals of Indian education (see Kessell 1976, 69, n. 10). He respected the aptitude and talent of his neophytes. Any teacher of basic design would understand the metaphor. Even if the design were an attempt at marbleizing—which seems highly improbable from the motifs shown in Fig. 13.III—the metaphor of "Indianizing" remains a valid hypothesis (see Barth 1950, 42, 54, 129, 362, and 375; Kubler 1972, 139).

8. Woodward, unfortunately, does not explain his observation, "Other evidences of reconstruction are seen in the addition of the bell tower." It seems

possible that he saw something, obvious in 1935, that has since been covered over or obliterated. Perhaps the building carcass might someday answer such questions as those raised by Woodward's casual remark.

9. In these last two paragraphs Woodward (as at San Valentín) inserts a moving soliloquy describing his subjective impressions at the site and adds a comparative review of Tubutama with several other missions he has recently visited.

Chapter 14. *Nuestra Señora de los Dolores*

1. Kino 1919, 1: 51–52 and 111.

2. Later in 1936, Woodward published his findings at the La Playa (Boquillas) site on the old Altar–Santa Ana highway (Woodward 1936a). This article reveals his extensive expertise in the field. Although not yet directly related to the missions, Woodward's findings are nevertheless of significance to archaeologists concerned with this region.

3. Stacy 1974.

4. In addition to the references cited in notes to chapter 1, n. 7, see Fontana et al. 1959; and Stacy 1974. Johnson 1960 was written on this site.

5. Having just completed an inspection of many mission locations, Woodward, in this résumé, offers a list of possible criteria for mission site selection, along with his idea of the probable extent of the complex in its heyday.

Chapter 15. *Los Santos Reyes de Cucurpe*

1. For a recent background study, "Cucurpe in Historical Perspective," see Sheridan 1988, 1–26.

2. See Reyes, "Report of 1772," 42–43. Reyes's description of this mission is somewhat more detailed than others; he was stationed here for over two years.

Chapter 16. *Los Santos Angeles de Guevavi (in Arizona)*

1. For an archaeological study of Guevavi with a section devoted to architecture see Robinson 1976. The history of Guevavi is detailed in Kessell 1970.

Chapter 17. *San Xavier del Bac (in Arizona)*

1. For a scholarly treatise on the sculpture and decorations see Ahlborn 1974. For a recent tribute to San Xavier del Bac, termed "The Queen of Sonora," see Banham 1982.

2. Except for Figs. 17.I and 17.II showing decorations for a comparison with similar examples in Sonora, DeLong and Miller did not include other drawings from either of the two Arizona mission churches, San Xavier del Bac or San José de Tumacácori. The former had already been published in 1919 and 1921 by Prentice Duell as cited by the authors. Today, San Xavier is probably the most

widely published Spanish colonial mission church in North America. For the lesser known, but significant, 1917 plan of Tumacacori by Duell, see Fig. B.2 in appendix B.

Chapter 18. Summary and Recommendations

1. For a more complete and recent study of manufacturing centers of majolica, see Lister and Lister 1987.

2. A summary of Tovrea's 1936 report is given in appendix B, pp. 157–162.

3. For a follow up of the architects' suggested color recording, see the published work of Steen and Gettens (1962).

4. This final paragraph is a reminder of the sparse literature "touching on" the architecture of Sonoran missions that was available in 1935: one book (1919) and a series of three magazine articles (1921) by an inspired graduate student at the University of Arizona, and one "picture book" (1901) covering the Spanish colonial architecture in all of Mexico.

5. It may seem ironic that Prentice Duell's "discovery" of Mission San Xavier del Bac, in 1917, ultimately resulted in such appropriate, world-wide acclaim, while the array of blood relations just across the border—also recognized by Duell and by Dr. Carl Russell of the National Park Service—have received little attention except as tourist attractions. But their authentic architecture and archaeology remain largely unstudied as part of the whole Pimería Alta mission field, with so much history common to all.

Appendix A

1. See AIA 1970. Also, see Harrison 1986, 430 and 433.

2. From AIA membership lists.

3. See Bailey 1959 for Woodward's bibliography to that date. Many works came later.

4. Sawyer 1986 contains a biographical sketch of Grant and reproductions of more than fifty of his western photographs.

5. See Tovrea and Pinkley 1936a, 1936b.

6. See diagram showing areas of excavation, Fig. B.3, in appendix B.

References

Authoritative books on the architecture and site plans of missions in northern Sonora are nonexistent. Three helpful guidebooks are included in the list below, each concerned primarily with the church as the mission: Polzer, *Kino Guide II* (1982), presents a concise biography of the founder, Padre Kino, with the religious and ethnological background of his Pimería Alta missions. Roca, *Paths of the Padres through Sonora* (1967), traces his own back-roads quest to locate the Sonoran churches. Also, he includes a well-researched history of the individuals related to them, seventy-seven pages of footnotes, and a fourteen-page bibliography. Eckhart and Griffith, *Temples in the Wilderness* (1975), is useful as a popular introduction to the subject.

None of these authors, however, professes to be concerned with mission architecture or archaeology per se. But as historical guidebooks, they do provide an essential reference—a point of departure—for the study of structure, design, and decoration (material culture data) presented here.

In addition to references used by Woodward (which are marked by an asterisk), the list below contains the publications and other works that have been useful in editing the text, photographs, maps, and drawings. Very few items are concerned with the total mission or the architecture; most are works that include scattered references or are cited in the foreword, introductions, appendices, or notes.

The two journal articles dealing with Sonoran architecture, Davis and Goss, "Cocóspera, Lonely Sentinel of Resurrection" (1977), and Goss, "The Churches of San Xavier and Caborca" (1975) are reviewed briefly in chapter 4, n. 12, and chapter 10, n. 7 respectively.

(Asterisks identify the items in Woodward's original 1936 bibliography.)

Ahlborn, Richard E. 1974. *The Sculpted Saints of a Borderland Mission: Los Bultos de San Xavier del Bac.* Tucson: Southwestern Mission Research Center.

Almada, Francisco. 1952. *Diccionario de historia, geografía y biografía sonorenses.* Chihuahua, Mexico: Ruiz Sandoval.

American Institute of Architects (AIA). 1970. *American Architects Directory.* 3d ed. New York: R. R. Bowker.

Anonymous. 1987. "On the 300-Year-Old Trail of Father Kino." *Sunset,* October, 52, 54, 56, 58.

Attwell, Walter G. 1937. "Excavation of Father Kino's Second Church and the Development of the Missions in Pimería Alta." Master's thesis, The University of Arizona, Tucson.

Bailey, Paul. 1959. "Arthur Woodward, Author: A Bibliography." *The Branding Iron,* no. 48. Los Angeles: The Los Angeles Corral of the Westerners.

Baird, Joseph A. 1962. *The Churches of Mexico: 1530–1810.* Berkeley: University of California Press.

Baldonado, Luis, OFM. 1959. "The Dedication of Caborca." *The Kiva* 24 (no. 4): inside back cover.

Bancroft, Hubert Howe. 1884–89. *History of the North Mexican States and Texas.* 2 vols. San Francisco: A.L. Bancroft.

*———. 1889. *History of Arizona and New Mexico, 1530–1888.* Vol. 12 of *The Works of Hubert Howe Bancroft.* San Francisco: The History Company.

Banham, Peter Reyner. 1982. "Mark on the Landscape." In *Scenes in America Deserta,* 171–79. Salt Lake City, Utah: A Peregrine Smith Book, Gibbs M. Smith.

Bannon, John Francis, SJ. 1955. *The Mission Frontier in Sonora, 1620–1687.* New York: United States Catholic Historical Society.

*Barber, Edwin Atlee. 1908. *The Majolica of Mexico.* Philadelphia: Pennsylvania Museum and School of Industrial Art.

Barth, Pius J., OFM. [1945] 1950. *Franciscan Education and the Social Order in Spanish North America, 1501–1821.* Chicago: De Paul University.

Bartlett, John Russell. 1854. *Personal Narrative of Explorations & Incidents in Texas, New Mexico, California, Sonora, and Chihuahua.* 2 vols. London: George Routledge & Co.

Baxter, Sylvester. 1901. *Spanish Colonial Architecture in Mexico.* 10 vols., folio. Boston.

*Beals, Ralph L. 1932. *The Comparative Ethnology of Northern Mexico before 1750.* Berkeley: University of California.

*———. 1934. "Material Culture of the Pima, Papago, and Western Apache." National Park Service, Field Division of Education, Berkeley. Mimeographed.

*———. 1935. "Preliminary Report on the Ethnology of the Southwest." National Park Service, Berkeley. Mimeographed.

Bleser, Nicholas J. 1989. *Tumacacori: from Ranchería to National Monument.* Tucson: Southwest Parks and Monuments Association.

Bolton, Herbert E. 1917. "The Mission as a Frontier Institution in the Spanish American Colonies." *American Historical Review* 23:42–61.

*———, translator and editor. 1919. *Kino's Historical Memoir of Pimería Alta.* 2 vols. Cleveland: Arthur H. Clark. (Supplemented by conversation with Bolton concerning certain items which I have noted in the body of my report. A.W.)

*———. 1930 [1966]. *Anza's California Expeditions.* 5 vols. Berkeley: University of California Press.

———. [1932] 1963. *Padre on Horseback.* Reprint with introduction by John Francis Bannon, sj. Chicago: Loyola University Press.

———. [1936 & 1960] 1984. *Rim of Christendom: A Biography of Eusebio Francisco Kino, Pacific Coast Pioneer.* Foreword by John L. Kessell. Tucson: The University of Arizona Press.

*Brand, Donald D. 1935. "The Distribution of Pottery Types in Northwest Mexico." *American Anthropologist* 37 (no. 2, pt. 1, April-June): 287–305.

Browne, J. Ross. 1869. *Adventures in the Apache Country: A Tour Through Arizona and Sonora, with Notes on the Silver Regions of Nevada.* New York: Harper & Brothers. Published in part as "A Tour through Arizona." *Harper's New Monthly Magazine* 29 (1864); and 30 (1865).

Browne, Lina Fergusson. 1969. *J. Ross Browne, His Letters and Writings.* Albuquerque: University of New Mexico Press.

Burrus, Ernest J., sj. 1965. *Kino and the Cartography of Northwestern New Spain.* Tucson: Arizona Pioneers' Historical Society.

———. 1971. *Kino and Manje, Explorers of Sonora and Arizona.* Rome and St. Louis: Jesuit Historical Institute.

Cheek, Annetta. 1974. "Evidence for Acculturation in Artifacts: Indians and Non-Indians at San Xavier del Bac, Arizona." Ph.D. dissertation, The University of Arizona, Tucson.

Cheek, Lawrence W. 1987. "The Kino Missions." *Arizona Highways*, September, 32–42.

*Cocóspera. "Los Libros de Bautismo y de Entierros, Santiago de Cocóspera, 1822–1836." Manuscript. Bancroft Library, University of California, Berkeley.

Crosby, Anthony. 1985. "Historic Structure Report, Tumacacori National Monument, Arizona." Denver, Colorado: Department of the Interior, National Park Service.

Cullimore, Clarence. 1954. "A California Martyr's Bones." *California Historical Society Quarterly* 33 (no. 1, March): 13–22.

Davis, Natalie Y., and Robert C. Goss. 1977. "Cocóspera, Lonely Sentinel of Resurrection." *El Palacio* 83 (no. 2): 25–40. (See mini-review, chapter 4, n. 12.)

Delbridge, Billy. 1928. "Inspecting Historic Missions." *Arizona Historical Review* 1 (no. 2, July): 85–92.

DeLong, Scofield, and Leffler B. Miller. [1936] 1976. "La Arquitectura de las Misiones de Sonora en la Pimería Alta." Translated and edited by Arturo Oliveros. In *El Valle de Cocóspera, Sonora. Primer Informe,* by Arturo Oliveros. Reprinted in *Cuadernos de los Centros,* no. 21 (March 1976), Part III. Mexico City: Dirección de Centros Regionales, Centro Regional del Noroeste, Instituto Nacional de Antropología e Historia.

Documentos para la historia de México, series 3, 1853–1857, 607, 617–37, and 838–42. Mexico City.

Donohue, John Augustine, sj. 1969. *After Kino, Jesuit Missions in Northwestern New Spain 1711–1767.* Rome and St. Louis: Jesuit Historical Institute.

Duell, Prentice. 1919. *Mission Architecture as Exemplified in San Xavier del Bac.* Tucson: Arizona Archaeological and Historical Society.

*———. 1921. "The Arizona-Sonora Chain of Missions." *The Architect and Engineer* 66 (July, September, and December).

Eckhart, George B., and James S. Griffith. 1975. *Temples in the Wilderness: The Spanish Churches of Northern Sonora.* Tucson: Arizona Historical Society.

*Englehardt, Zephyrin, ofm. 1899. *The Franciscans in Arizona.* Harbor Springs, Michigan: Holy Childhood Indian School.

*Ewing, Russell Charles. 1934. "The Pima Uprising 1751–1752." Ph.D. dissertation, University of California, Berkeley.

Fireman, Janet R. 1977. *The Spanish Royal Corps of Engineers in the Western Borderlands, Instrument of Bourbon Reform 1764–1815.* Glendale, California: Arthur H. Clark Co.

Fontana, Bernard L. 1961. "Biography of a Desert Church: the Story of Mission San Xavier del Bac." *The Smoke Signal,* no. 3: 1–24. Tucson: Tucson Corral of the Westerners. Reprinted 1971.

———. 1981a. *Of Earth and Little Rain: The Papago Indians.* Flagstaff, Arizona: Northland Press.

———. 1981b. "Pilgrimage to Magdalena." *The American West* 18 (no. 5): 40–45, and 60.

———. 1983. "Pima and Papago: Introduction." In *Southwest,* edited by Alfonso Ortiz, 125–36. Vol. 10 of *Handbook of North American Indians.* Washington, D.C.: Smithsonian Institution.

———. 1987. "Santa Ana de Cuiquiburitac: Pimería Alta's Northernmost Mission." *Journal of the Southwest* 29:133–59.

Fontana, Bernard L., J. Cameron Greenleaf, and Donnelly D. Cassidy. 1959. "A Fortified Arizona Mountain." *The Kiva* 25 (no. 2): 41–53.

Fontana, Bernard L. et al. 1962. *Papago Indian Pottery.* Monographs of The American Ethnological Society No. 37. Seattle: University of Washington Press.

Forbes, Robert H. 1952. *Crabb's Filibustering Expedition into Sonora, 1857.* Tucson: Arizona Silhouettes.

Fratt, Lee. 1986. "Tumacacori National Monument: Archeological Assessment and Management Recommendations." In *Miscellaneous Historic Period Archeological Projects in the Western Region*, 42–74. Publications in Anthropology No. 37. Tucson: Western Archeological and Conservation Center.

Gerald, Rex E. 1966. "Portrait of a Community, Joseph de Urrutia's Map of El Paso del Norte, 1766." *The American West* 3:38–41.

———. 1968. *Spanish Presidios of the Late Eighteenth Century in Northern New Spain*. Santa Fe: Museum of New Mexico Press.

Goss, Robert C. 1975. "The Churches of San Xavier, Arizona and Caborca, Sonora, A Comparative Analysis." *The Kiva* 40 (no. 3): 165–79. (See mini-review, chapter 10, n. 7.)

Griffith, James S. 1989. "Tracking Father Kino by Time Machine." *Tucson Guide* 37 (no. 4, Winter): 54–57. Tucson: Madden Publishing.

Harrison, Laura Soullière. 1986. "Tumacacori Museum." In *Architecture in the Parks, National Historic Landmark Theme Study*, 425–39. Washington, D.C.: Department of the Interior, National Park Service.

*Hernandez, Lamberto. 1926. *Datos históricos sobre los filibusteros de 1857 en Caborca, Sonora, México*. Mexico City.

Hinton, Thomas B. 1955. "A Survey of Archaeological Sites in the Altar Valley, Sonora." *The Kiva* 21 (nos. 1–2): 1–12.

*Hodge, F. W., editor. 1907–10. *Handbook of the American Indians North of Mexico*. 2 vols. Washington, D.C.: Government Printing Office.

Ivey, James E. 1988. "The Structural History of the Salinas Missions." Historic Structures Report. National Park Service, Southwest Regional Office, Santa Fe, New Mexico.

Johnson, Alfred E. 1960. "The Place of the Trincheras Culture in Northern Sonora in Southwestern Archaeology." Master's thesis, University of Arizona, Tucson.

———. 1963–1964. "The Trincheras Culture of Northern Sonora." *American Antiquity* 29 (no. 2): 74–186.

Kelemen, Pál. 1951, 1967. *Baroque and Rococo in Latin America*. New York: Macmillan. Reprinted in 2 vols. New York: Dover Publications.

———. 1977. *Vanishing Art of the Americas*. New York: Walker & Company.

———. 1979. *Stepchild of the Humanities: Art of the Americas, as Observed in Five Decades*. Tucson: Southwestern Mission Research Center.

Kessell, John L. 1970. *Mission of Sorrows: Jesuit Guevavi and the Pimas, 1691–1767*. Tucson: The University of Arizona Press.

———. 1976. *Friars, Soldiers, and Reformers: Hispanic Arizona and the Sonora Mission Frontier, 1767–1856*. Tucson: The University of Arizona Press.

———. 1980. *The Missions of New Mexico Since 1776*. Albuquerque: University of New Mexico Press.

Kino, Eusebio Francisco, sj. 1919, 1948. *Kino's Historical Memoir of Pimería Alta.* Translated and edited by Herbert E. Bolton. 2 vols. Cleveland: Arthur H. Clark. Reprinted as 2 vols. in one. Berkeley and Los Angeles: University of California Press.

————. 1971. *Kino's Biography of Francisco Javier Saeta, S.J.* Translated and edited by Charles W. Polzer, with the original Spanish text edited by Ernest J. Burrus. Rome and St. Louis: Jesuit Historical Institute.

Konrad, Herman W. 1980. *A Jesuit Hacienda in Colonial Mexico, Santa Lucía, 1576–1767.* Stanford, California: Stanford University Press.

Kubler, George. [1940] 1972. *Religious Architecture of New Mexico.* Albuquerque: University of New Mexico Press.

————. 1943, 1983, 1985. "Two Modes of Franciscan Architecture: New Mexico and California." *Gazette des Beaux-Arts,* 6th series, 23 (no. 911, January): 39–48. Reprinted in *Franciscan Studies in the Americas,* Academy of American Franciscan Studies, 369–75; also in *Studies in Ancient American and European Art: The Collected Essays of George Kubler,* edited by Thomas F. Reese, 34–38. New Haven: Yale University Press.

————. 1944. "Architects and Builders in Mexico: 1521–1550." *Journal of the Warburg and Courtauld Institutes* 7:7–19. London: The Warburg Institute.

————. 1948. *Mexican Architecture of the Sixteenth Century.* 2 vols. New Haven: Yale University Press.

————. 1985. "The Arts, Fine and Plain." In *Studies in Ancient American and European Art: The Collected Essays of George Kubler,* edited by Thomas F. Reese, 111–17. New Haven: Yale University Press.

Lister, Florence C., and Robert H. Lister. 1987. *Andalusian Ceramics in Spain and New Spain.* Tucson: The University of Arizona Press.

*Lockwood, Frank C. 1934a. *Story of the Spanish Missions of the Middle Southwest.* Santa Ana, California: Fine Arts Press.

————. 1934b. "With Padre Kino on the Trail." *University of Arizona Bulletin* 5 (no. 2); *Social Science Bulletin,* no. 5. Tucson: The University of Arizona.

McCarty, Kieran, ofm. 1976a. *Desert Documentary: the Spanish Years, 1767–1821.* Tucson: Arizona Historical Society.

————. 1976b. "A History of Construction at Tubutama." Letter to Arturo Oliveros. (Copy to editor courtesy of Dr. Bernard Fontana.)

————. 1981. *A Spanish Frontier in the Enlightened Age, Franciscan Beginnings in Sonora and Arizona, 1767–1770.* Washington, D.C.: Academy of American Franciscan History.

McDermott, Edwin J. 1961. "The Saga of Father Kino." *Arizona Highways,* March, 6–29.

McGuire, Randall H. 1984. "Las trincheras prospeción proyecto trabajo del campo–Verano." Nineteen-page typescript. State University of New York, Binghamton. Copy on file at the Arizona State Museum, Tucson.

McGuire, Randall H., and M. Elisa Villalpando. 1989. "Prehistory and the Making of History in Sonora." In *Archaeology of the Spanish Borderlands.* Vol. 1, edited by D. H. Thomas, 157–77. Washington, D.C.: Smithsonian Institution.

Matson, Daniel S., and Bernard L. Fontana. 1977. *Friar Bringas Reports to the King.* Tucson: The University of Arizona Press.

Mills, Hazel. 1932. "Jacobo Sedelmayr: A Jesuit in Pimería Alta, 1736–1767." Master's thesis, University of California, Berkeley.

Moorhead, Max L. 1975. *The Presidio, Bastion of the Spanish Borderlands.* Norman: University of Oklahoma Press.

Nentwig, Juan, sj. [1764] 1980. *Rudo Ensayo: A Description of Sonora and Arizona in 1764.* Translated by Albert F. Pradeau and Robert R. Rasmussen. Tucson: The University of Arizona Press.

Neuerburg, Norman. 1987. *The Decoration of the California Missions.* Santa Barbara, California: Bellerophon Books.

*Ocaranza, Fernando. 1933. *Los Franciscanos en las Provincias Internas de Sonora y Ostimuri, (misiones en Pimería Alta y Baja).* México. [Added by A.W. in his *Misiones del Norte de Sonora* (1983).]

Ortiz, Alfonso, editor. 1983. *Southwest.* Vol. 10 of *Handbook of North American Indians,* general editor William C. Sturtevant. Washington, D.C.: Smithsonian Institution.

Peterson, Charles E. 1957. "The Historic American Buildings Survey Continued." *Journal of the Society of Architectural Historians* 16 (no. 3, October): 29–31.

Pfefferkorn, Ignaz, sj. [1795] 1949. *Sonora: A Description of the Province.* Translated by Theodore E. Treutlein. Albuquerque: University of New Mexico Press.

Pinart, Alphonse. 1962. *Journey to Arizona in 1876.* Translated from the French by George H. Whitney. Los Angeles: The Zamorano Club.

Pinkley, Frank, and J. H. Tovrea. 1936a. "The Tumacacori Choir Loft Problem." *Southwestern Monuments Monthly Report,* supplement for May: 375–78; also *Southwestern Monuments Special Report,* no. 4 (May). Coolidge, Arizona: Department of the Interior, National Park Service.

———. 1936b. "Tumacacori Alcoves or Transepts." *Southwestern Monuments Monthly Report,* supplement for August: 121–25; also *Southwestern Monuments Special Report,* no. 9 (August). Coolidge, Arizona: Department of the Interior, National Park Service.

Polzer, Charles W., sj. [1968, 1972, 1976] 1982. *Kino Guide II, A Life of Eusebio Francisco Kino, S.J., Arizona's First Pioneer, and A Guide to His Missions and Monuments.* Tucson: Southwestern Mission Research Center.

*Rensch, H. E. C. 1934. "Chronology for Tumacacori National Monument." National Park Service, Field Division of Education, Berkeley. Mimeographed.

Reyes, Antonio María de los, OFM. "Reyes Report of 1772, A report on the existing conditions in the Missions of Sonora administered by the Fathers of the Propagation of the Faith College of the Holy Cross in Querétaro, Mexico." Manuscript, edited and translated, n.d., by Kieran McCarty, OFM. Copy on file in the Oblasser Memorial Library, Mission San Xavier del Bac, Tucson.

Ricard, Robert. [1933] 1966. *The Spiritual Conquest of Mexico.* Translated by Lesley B. Simpson. Berkeley: University of California Press.

Robinson, William J. 1963. "Excavations at San Xavier del Bac, 1958." *The Kiva* 29 (no. 2): 35–57.

———. 1976. "Mission Guevavi: Excavations in the Convento." *The Kiva* 42 (no. 2): 135–75.

Roca, Paul M. 1967. *Paths of the Padres through Sonora: An Illustrated History and Guide to Its Spanish Churches.* Tucson: Arizona Pioneers' Historical Society.

———. 1979. *Spanish Jesuit Churches in Mexico's Tarahumara.* Tucson: The University of Arizona Press.

Rose, Robert H. 1936. "Bancroft Library Research." *Southwestern Monuments Monthly Report,* supplement for November: 335–56, and supplement for December: 413–36. Coolidge, Arizona: Department of the Interior, National Park Service.

Rothman, Hal. 1989. "Boss Pinkley's Domain." In *Preserving Different Pasts: The American National Monuments,* 119–40. Urbana: University of Illinois Press.

Ruibal Corella, Juan Antonio. 1976. *¡y Caborca se cubrio de gloria!* México: Editorial Porrúa.

Russell, Carl P. 1935. "The Tumacacori Story." Typescript. Library item no. 4691, National Park Service, Western Archeological and Conservation Center, Tucson.

Sauer, Carl, and Donald Brand. 1931. "Prehistoric Settlements of Sonora, with Special Reference to Cerros de Trincheras." *University of California Publications in Geography* 5 (no. 3): 67–148. Berkeley.

Sawyer, Mark. 1986. *Early Days: Photographer George Alexander Grant and the Western National Parks.* Flagstaff, Arizona: Northland Press.

Schroeder, Albert H. 1957. "Comments on San Cayetano de Tumacácori." Manuscript. National Park Service, Globe, Arizona.

Schuetz, Mardith K. 1983. "Professional Artisans in the Hispanic Southwest." *The Americas* 40: 17–71. Bethesda, Maryland: Academy of American Franciscan History.

———, translator and editor. 1987. *Architectural Practice in Mexico City: A Manual for Journeyman Architects of the Eighteenth Century.* Tucson: The University of Arizona Press.

Sheridan, Thomas E. 1988. *Where the Dove Calls: The Political Ecology of a Peasant Corporate Community in Northwestern Mexico.* Tucson: The University of Arizona Press.

Spence, Jonathan O. 1984. *The Memory Palace of Matteo Ricci.* New York: Viking Press.

Stacy, Valeria K. P. 1974. "Cerros de Trincheras in the Arizona Papaquería." Ph.D. dissertation, The University of Arizona, Tucson.

Steen, Charles R., and Rutherford J. Gettens. 1962. "Tumacacori Interior Decorations." *Arizoniana* 3:7–21. Tucson: Arizona Pioneers' Historical Society.

Thybony, Scott. 1989. "Under the Bells: The Spanish Missions of Father Kino." *National Geographic Traveler* 6 (no. 1, January/February): 50–62.

Toussaint, Manuel. 1967. *Colonial Art in Mexico.* Translated and edited by Elizabeth Wilder Weismann. Austin and London: University of Texas Press.

Tovrea, J. H. 1936. "Report on Mission San José de Tumacácori." *Southwestern Monuments Monthly Report,* supplement for January: 41–54. Coolidge, Arizona: Department of the Interior, National Park Service.

Tovrea, J. H., and Frank Pinkley. 1936a. "The Tumacacori Choir Loft Problem." *Southwestern Monuments Monthly Report,* supplement for May: 375–78; also *Southwestern Monuments Special Report,* no. 4 (May). Coolidge, Arizona: Department of the Interior, National Park Service.

————. 1936b. "Tumacacori Alcoves or Transepts." *Southwestern Monuments Monthly Report,* supplement for August: 121–25; also *Southwestern Monuments Special Report*, no. 9 (August). Coolidge, Arizona: Department of the Interior, National Park Service.

Trailer, A. 1921. "Along Untrodden Trails." *Franciscan Herald* 9 (no. 8, June): 241–44. Chicago: Friars Minor of the Sacred Heart Province.

Treutlein, Theodore E., translator and editor. 1965. *Missionary in Sonora: The Travel Reports of Joseph Och, S.J., 1755–1767.* San Francisco: California Historical Society.

*Velarde, Luis, Padre, sj. 1931. "Relation de la Pimería Alta." Translated and edited by Rufus Kay Wyllus. *New Mexico Historical Review* 7 (no. 2, April).

Wasley, William W. [1965] 1976. "Cronología Preliminar para las Misiones del Padre Kino: Nuestra Señora de los Remedios y Nuestra Señora del Pilar y Santiago de Cocóspera." Translated by Arturo Oliveros. In *El Valle de Cocóspera, Sonora. Primer Informe,* by Arturo Oliveros. Reprinted in *Cuadernos de los Centros,* no. 21 (March 1976), Part II. Mexico City: Dirección de Centros Regionales, Centro Regional del Noroeste, Instituto Nacional de Antropología e Historia.

Weismann, Elizabeth Wilder. 1985. *Art and Time in Mexico from the Conquest to the Revolution.* New York, Cambridge, Philadelphia, San Francisco, London, Mexico City, Sao Paulo, Singapore, and Sydney: Icon editions, Harper & Row.

Whiffen, Marcus. 1970. Review of *Paths of the Padres Through Sonora: An Illustrated History and Guide to Its Spanish Churches,* by Paul M. Roca. *Journal of the Society of Architectural Historians* 29 (no. 2, May): 201–2.

Williams, Jack S. 1986a. "San Augustín del Tucson: A Vanished Mission Community of the Pimería Alta." *The Smoke Signal,* no. 47: 112–28. Tucson: Tucson Corral of the Westerners.

———. 1986b. "The Presidio of Santa Cruz de Terrenate: A Forgotten Fortress of Southern Arizona." *The Smoke Signal,* no. 48: 129–48. Tucson: Tucson Corral of the Westerners.

———. 1988. "Fortress Tucson: Architecture and the Art of War (1775–1856)." *The Smoke Signal,* no. 50: 168–87. Tucson: Tucson Corral of the Westerners.

Woodward, Arthur. 1933. "Ancient Houses of Modern Mexico." *Southern California Academy of Sciences Bulletin* 32 (pt. 3).

———. 1936a. "A Shell Bracelet Manufactory." *American Antiquity* 2:117–25.

———. 1936b. "Tentative Exhibit Plan for a New Museum at Tumacacori National Monument." Typescript. Library item no. 4691. National Park Service, Western Archeological and Conservation Center, Tucson.

———. [1938] 1946. "A Brief History of Navajo Silversmithing." *Museum of Northern Arizona Bulletin,* no. 14. Flagstaff, Arizona.

———. 1970. *The Denominators of the Fur Trade: An Anthology of Writings on the Material Culture of the Fur Trade.* Pasadena, California: Socio-Technical Publications.

———. 1983. *Misiones del norte de Sonora. Aspectos históricos y arqueológicos.* Prólogo de Charles W. Polzer. Hermosillo: Gobierno del Estado de Sonora. (A Spanish translation of Woodward's previously unpublished 1936 report, the original presented here in English).

Index

ABOUT THE EDITOR

Buford L. Pickens is a Fellow of the American Institute of Architects; he has been a practicing architect in private practice. Former positions he has held include Director of the School of Architecture at Tulane University and Dean of the School of Architecture at Washington University as well as a teacher at Ohio University, Wayne State University, the University of Minnesota, and in Florence, Italy.

He has served on committees concerned with the protection of historic buildings in New Orleans, in the State of Missouri, and in St. Louis County, Missouri. He has also had significant involvement with the Historic American Buildings Survey and with the National Trust for Historic Preservation.

Pickens has contributed to three books and is author of nearly four dozen articles on architecture and architectural history published in professional journals. Today he lives in Webster Groves, Missouri, and is a Professor Emeritus in Architecture at Washington University in St. Louis.